THE
ONE-TERM
SOLUTION

* * *

Ending the evils of reelection
and politics as a career

* * *

by
Kent Welton

Pandit Press Inc.

THE ONE-TERM SOLUTION

A Pandit Press Book

- PRINTING HISTORY -
Pandit Press Edition published November 1988

Pandit Press Inc.
P.O. Box 7200
1548-D Adams Ave.
Costa Mesa, Ca. 92626

Printed in the United States of America
ISBN# 0-944361-25-0
CIP# 88-062939

"A new science of politics is needed for a new world."

Alexis De Tocqueville

iv

FORWARD

It is no longer possible to deny the scandal inherent in modern american politics. Whether on the local, state, or national level our crisis in political representation is real and seemingly impervious to effective reform. Political analysts are only now beginning to question the very foundations of our mode of political representation and increasingly concluding that systemic corruption and failure is bred by the very structure of modern elective politics. Essentially, our political system, as it stands today, is subverted by the machinations of re-electable career politicians.

The sorry results of a campaign finance and reelection system gone wrong, virtually creating conflicts-of-interest for our representatives, is everywhere evident in our political process. We have only to consider the recent spectacle of Congress deciding the level of their own salaries and perquisites while at the same time exempting itself from the Ethics in Government Act and numerous other laws setting standards for everyone, it seems, but Congress itself. And this breakdown in political administration is annually displayed when the federal government itself is held hostage at budget time by our "representatives" with 1000-page continuing resolutions filled with legislators pet pork-barrel projects, and purposely passed on the last day of the fiscal year to prevent debate and cuts by the Executive Branch.

In a larger context, we have only to examine the world around us, and our burgeoning future obligations, to conclude our political system is not meeting the challenge. Witness our progression from a creditor to a debtor nation, with interest payments alone now taking an alarming percentage of our total revenues; a mindless mistreatment of the natural ecosystems creating a lethal and cancerous environment; continual destruction of virgin landscape and once beautiful and balanced neighborhoods; abysmal failures to provide effective rapld transit; and a gradual and real decline in both quality of life and our standards of living brought about, in large part, by misguided and corrupt political activity.

At all levels of government today the abuses of entrenched, and conflicted, political power continue unabated. But no less than radical political surgery, by the people, will improve our defective system of representation. The very security of our immediate future now depends on effective political reform. As it stands the political process is not only rotten but lethal.

However, in order to consider options to the current system of elective politics we must first understand where we, as a nation, have come from and where we are likely headed if serious and fundamental political reform is not forthcoming. The purpose of this study is not only to inquire into the framers original rational regarding elective office, but also to examine why a radical change in our political ethic is both possible and necessary.

The political power of the american people comes out of the barrel of our constitution - thru the use of the amendment and initiative process. This book is dedicated to the growing legion of citizen-politicians who will soon be forced to use these very processes to not only rescue our future but to recapture as well the true integrity and spirit of the political process and elevate the art of participation in government.

K.W.

— TABLE OF CONTENTS —

CHAPTER IV - CAREERS AND CORRUPTION

CHAPTER V - "WE, THE PEOPLE"

CHAPTER VI - JUSTICE FOR SALE

CHAPTER VII - THE MEDIA AND POLITICS

CHAPTER VIII - CONCLUSIONS AND RECOMMENDATIONS

CHAPTER I

"THE COMMON GOOD"

"The aim of every political constitution is, or ought to be, first to obtain for rulers men who possess most wisdom to discern, and most virtue to pursue, the common good of the society; and in the next place, to take the most effectual precautions for keeping them virtuous whilst they continue to hold their public trust... The elective mode of obtaining rulers is the characteristic policy of republican government. The means relied on in this form of government for preventing their degeneracy are numerous and various. The most effectual one is such a limitation of the term of appointments as will maintain a proper responsibility to the people."[1]

James Madison

Good government is essential to the preservation of our political freedoms and economic prosperity. But no republic, or democracy, endures without encountering periods of inferior and inadequate government that may ultimately jeopardize its very existence. Today the deleterious effects of pervasive political campaign finance corruption, and near-perpetual incumbency, upon the most significant legislative issues of our time are reason enough to re-examine the structure and rational behind our traditional political institutions.

It is obvious the nature and scope of political "reform" to date has not solved our problems, or prevented degeneracy in political representation. Only the most idealistic could believe we might one day transform the human political animal. It is clear that the people's only realistic alternative is to redesign the elective political process around the defects of human nature if we are to improve our system of government.

The problem with past "reform" legislation is that it has rarely penetrated to the essential motivations underlying abuse of power, influence, corruption, and prolonged incumbency. In addition, recent reform legislation has not properly addressed the perils of underlying structural problems which, when combined with an essentially unprogressive human nature, give us what we have today. Future political reform efforts must proceed from an understanding of how our current election system affects chances for geniune change. Otherwise, voters have little chance of reforming special-interest corruption, dismantling legislative gridlock, and bringing an end to the cult of the incumbent.

There is little question that an alert and active citizenry is the first line of defense against the inevitable encroachment of government upon our freedoms and responsibilities. Like water, political power and influence flow inevitably into all areas left unprotected by a less than vigilant body politic. But fortunately we are blessed with a constitution enabling the voting public either directly, or thru elected representatives, to continue to alter and experiment with their political institutions to meet the needs of the time.

There is no denying that the republic for which we stand, the United States of America, is ultimately an ongoing experiment in the allocation of power to the people. And, as James Madison recognized, the selection of optimum modes of representation is of prime importance in assuring the lasting success of our american political experiment. However, there is no denying the proposition that political and economic circumstances may change with the passage of time. The changes wrought over two hundred years, along with the introduction of new technology, have given new meaning to the document that governs our political existence.

Our local, state, and national governments are held hostage today in yet another crisis of corruption brought about by the rapid and obscene growth of the political power of incumbents, in concert with the spread of vote-buying and influence peddling by powerful special-interest groups. It is this new and powerful equation defining the terms of the current structure of political representation and elective systems, when combined with the new and absolute power of money and media, that has fundamentally altered the balance of power between government and the governed.

We live in a different "United States" from that inhabited by the designers of our constitution. In some ways our charter no longer addresses our political needs. The very foundations of beneficial government, of good and virtuous representation, have now been corrupted beyond the wildest dreams of the framers. The modern day spectacle of candidates seeking, and taking, enormous sums of money to pay campaign expenses, virtually guaranteeing reelection for most incumbents, has turned the art of politics into a truly sordid affair. We have lost our way.

But until we appreciate the substantial differences between the world we live in today, and that which existed when our constitution was written, we may not fully realize the need for a review of our political institutions. However, once voters comprehend the real reasons behind the collapse of beneficial representation they will be moved to change the system. But whatever form those changes may take, it is increasingly likely that our political figures across the Potomac, and the nation, will soon feel the sting of the second American Constitutional Revolution.

"The tyranny of legislators is at present, and will be for many years, our most formidable danger."[2]

Thomas Jefferson

Despite Jefferson's centuries-old warning, we have yet to ask the right questions about our system of representation. Once we do, however, the only debate left about political reform

3

will be over what form changes will take. Still, a vital question remains whether a majority of Americans now have the inclination and political will to challenge and change our current system.

Obviously, voters have not deliberately set out to lose control of their government and representatives? But corruption and legislative tyranny is the essence of our situation today. With this in mind, we must ask whether elections today serve any useful purpose?

What results do elections, and reelections, produce? Or, perhaps more accurately, what mischief do they inspire?

Due to the modern consequences of the design defects in our system of representation, perhaps unforeseen by the founding fathers, future generations of Americans will suffer the mounting costs of our continuing political corruption and legislative gridlock. The costs to Americans of soaring budget deficits (in amounts unimagined just a few years ago) along with the hidden taxation of de-facto currency devaluation, a lowering of living standards, and an unprecented assault upon our natural environment, will ultimately mandate another revolution in American politics.

We are now over 200 years into our political experiment, called the United States of America, and there is good reason to ask why are so many of our domestic problems keep getting worse, even multiplying in their ramifications rather than improving and diminishing in effect? Too few examples of that elusive concept called "progress" are evident in our political, economic, and environmental affairs? Where are we headed?

Why has our real standard of living declined for the last twenty years? Why, in view of the knowledge of our problems, has there been further deterioration of our eco-system and living environments? Why has our federal deficit mushroomed to staggering heights without effective control? Why, despite the promise of technology and twenty-first century miracles, do we now appear to be on the edge of an economic, social, and environmental abyss? Why, despite legions of "professional" career legislators in our employ can we not solve our problems?

Indeed, what have voters gained, or lost, from the last generation of political leaders? And, working within the current political context, what will we likely gain or lose from the next? Given our status quo, what does this legislative gridlock on our many pressing problems portend?

Further reform is imperative. The dangers of unlimited incumbency, a candidate's massive media dependency, and the largely uncontrolled special-interest group process of campaign financing are reason enough to make us wonder about our future.

Unfortunately, as most governments age and grow in size they also seem to degenerate. As a mature nation, in its post-imperial years, the United States is now plagued with a behomoth bureaucracy and reelectable politicians dependent upon special-interests. We appear to "lurch from crisis to crisis" and suffer the stalemates common to manipulated government. Our problems fester while the election circus continues.

The theme of this book is that the people of the United States have now arrived at a time and circumstance demanding a thorough re-examination of the fundamentals of participation in politics, as well as the effects upon our government bodies of the reelection process itself.

One of our main constitutional theorists, James Madison, believed that the "means" relied on to "prevent degeneracy" in our form of government are many and varied. There is no question the constitutional powers of the people are already in place. And short of revolution, it is a historical fact that governments and legislatures seldom reform themselves. However, the ways and means provided for constitutional reform are only valuable if they are utilized.

In other words, we must have the will to use our charter to our best advantage. We, the people, must exercise our right to make systemic changes in our election processes by utilizing the people power of the constitution. Whether by constitutional amendment, national initiative, or other means, change must come. However cumbersome, we are fortunate that we have in place the framework and means to institute radical political

5

surgery and bypass our current "elected" representatives when the need arises. And human nature being what it is, reform must come from outside our legislatures. Reform must "trickle-up" from the electorate. A one-term solution must come from the people.

There have been numerous occasions in our political history when, due to legislative gridlock, the need has arisen to amend the constitution. Once again it is apparent the time has come to revitalize American politics with certain fundamental changes in our system of representation. When government breaks down, due to the self-interests of politicians and their campaign financiers, solutions to our myriad problems remain at bay - and progress is delayed or buried. This state of affairs fairly characterizes our present situation.

History provides us with ample evidence of the dangers of a class of professional "career" politicians and bureaucrats. In fact, the decline of good and vital government, and the rise of professional politicians, appear to go hand in hand. And all political revolutions, bloody or benign, begin when legislative impasse becomes intractable and the people sense the building of a new political tyranny.

Examples of the unsalutary effects of the ascendence of a professional political class are provided by the ancient Greek and Roman imperial governments - powerful nation-states not unlike our own. In an ascerbic and biting letter to a colleague, circa 54 B.C., Cicero described the prevailing state of affairs in the waning days of Imperial Rome:

> "Now let's look at the polls, bribery's thriving. I'll give you a sign: since July 15, the interest rate has doubled... Caesar is backing Memmius with all his might... in a deal I don't dare put in writing. Pompey is fuming and growling and backing Scaurus, but who knows whether as a front or for real. None is ahead; their handouts are keeping them all even."[3]

Some twenty centuries later, little has changed in the political arena since Cicero's day. This same "pork barrel" political ethic is alive today and leading us down a similar path of decline. Are we headed in the same direction as the older bygone empires of western history? I think so. Until we act upon the underlying causes of the increasing failure of our local, state, and national governments to come to terms with the great social, economic, and environmental problems of our time we are doomed to repeat the folly of the past.

To the extent a disallusioned and dispirited electorate delegates their political responsibilities to representatives who grow fond of their special status, power, and political career, they have set the stage for calamity. Replacing ethics and integrity in our legislatures will be as difficult as restoring the value of our currency. Great nations do not decay overnight but gradually lose vitality, as coins are clipped, and public institutions are usurped by legions of careerists - a monopoly that sucks dry the remaining political instincts of the body politic. Inevitably, the self-interests of career politicians and bureaucrats replace the legitimate interests of the society as a whole. And this is precisely our problem today.

The dialectic is clear - decline is inevitable if the political dynamics of great nations follow a predictable pattern of growing disinterest and indifference amongst the voting public, while at the same time spawning a cadre of professional politicians with reelection and self-preservation at the top of the agenda. Today, increasing faction, hollow reform efforts, and legislative paralysis will likely continue until some form of people's revolution becomes the "final solution" to our problems. And without workable and effective political reform eventually the most odious of "solutions" are likely to surface under the banner of necessity.

In a 1972 critique entitled "Who Runs Congress" Ralph Nader, an exemplary public activist, passionately defined our modern political dilemma: He stated "there should be little disagreement over the assertion that ours is a society of unparalleled material wealth and skill, increasingly unable to solve, diminish, or forestall problems to which wealth and skill should be responsive. This gnawing paradox is a signal fact of contemporary American life - one with worldwide repercussion. As our dollar Gross National Product (GNP) zooms upward, our cities are rotting, malnutrition and disease stalk millions of impoverished citizens, pollution is increasing faster than GNP; the narcotics trade eats at the human fiber; government corruption and waste are bursting out all over; bureaucracy has become the opiate of the people; consumer fraud accelerates hand in hand with Big Business domination of the economy and much of government; rank-and-file disgruntlement with labor leadership deepens; and housing, rapid transit, and medical care seem to defy even a focused effort at resolution."[4]

Nearly two decades later, little has changed and Nader's indictment stands intact. Increasingly, a political ennui has spread amongst our disallusioned and now largely semi-literate electorate. Indeed, bureaucracy has become the opiate of the people.

Could it be we have a defect in our electoral system?

Is there a new and unique virus loose in modern politics unforeseen by the framers of our constitution?

Or have we simply programmed our eventual demise into our system of government and representation?

And has the passage of time, along with the impact of critical events and new technology, simply made a mockery of our forefather's vision and intent?

In looking back to our first Constitutional Convention, it was a curious lot of merchants, farmers, and landed gentry who traveled from the distant towns of the thirteen colonies to Philadelphia, in the sweltering summer of 1787, for the purpose of writing a constitution for a new federation of states. The writers of our constitution were, for the most part, not what one would call career politicians, lobbyists, bureaucrats, or weak quislings of anybody's court. On the whole a young group, with an average age of forty-two, they comprised an assembly of mostly well-to-do and fiercely independent generalists flavored with a few even more free-spirited frontier populists.

Although largely a privileged lot, they were by no means political neophytes as nearly all of the sixty plus delegates, elected by their respective states to attend the Constitutional Convention, had at some time been on the public payroll in an elective or appointive capacity. There were judges, legislators, and even governors in attendance, many of whom had participated in the writing of their state own constitutions.

Given the writers of the American Constitution were not new to politics, neither were they professional politicians as we know them today. And dispite the disengagement from the mother country brought on by the revolution, they were not tied by tradition to implacable parties or factions. They had a common bond - they were worried about writing a workable constitution, and not reelection.

These were men of goodwill who came together with the interests of the nation, above all, at heart. And even after a divisive revolutionary war, in which a number of "tories" sided with the British, they joined together to form "a more perfect union." And when the political and civic work of constructing a nation was complete they could return to their homes and normal livelihoods. Thus, while civic participation was considered a duty in the early days of our republic, the idea of a life-long career in politics was likely foreign and repulsive to the early colonists who had only recently escaped from a long and stagnant tradition of oppressive bureaucracy. Politics was more nearly synonymous with service, a responsibilty of mature citizens, and an honor not to be taken lightly.

Sadly, however, this ideal does not seem to be the case today. Until the advent of the modern industrial state, a gentlemanly participation in government was more the rule than the exception in the normal course of affairs. The idea of a "career" in government, by itself, was considered strange if not altogether suspect. However, a healthy participation in politics was part and parcel of the spirit of the times, as well as an integral part of the social milieu of the "upper" class.

Coming from our revolutionary days, how is it we have today cultured and continued a system built upon the politics of the ego and the cult of career self-aggrandisement? Just what has happened to the principle of selfless service in government by those who had reached maturity and economic stability? As voters we must ask ourselves why we continue to encourage and pay for politicians whose primary aim is to contruct a self-perpetuating political career at public expense?

Why do so many politicians today never voluntarily leave office once elected? Why have we allowed the current power of incumbents to become so overwhelming and ultimately destructive to our political and economic health? Indeed, why have our societal problems only multiplied and become more intractable in the era of the specialist, the "professional" politician?

"THE RIGHT OF THE PEOPLE" —

"I trust the friends of the constitution will never concur with its enemies in questioning that fundamental principle of republican government which admits the right of the people to alter or abolish the established constitution whenever they find it inconsistent with their happiness."[5]

Alexander Hamilton

* * *

"Whenever any Form of Government becomes destructive, it is the Right of the People to alter or abolish it."[6]

Declaration of Independence

There is good reason to believe that Hamilton and other writers of our Contitution would be more than alarmed could they somehow witness our present state of affairs. Realizing the future might well bring such change and the need for new reform, James Madison suggested that "in framing a system which we wish to last for ages we should not lose sight of

10

the changes the ages will produce." And the ages have indeed produced changes.

Is there a better way? How can voters begin to extricate themselves from an election system now proving inpenetrable to anyone but incumbents, so well-endowed with the frank and the hefty perquisites of public power and media exposure? And short of a system overhaul, must we be doomed to a treadmill of continuously re-electing incumbents simply because of their ready access to media and ability to raise funds throughout their term? Is it our political fate, in perpetuity, to be stuck with slowly-revolving crowds of ambitious and self-perpetuating political representatives whose livelihood depends on a public salary? Is this our Hobson's choice?

To date, americans have shyed away from fine-tuning their constitution and political institutions. Revolution and reform are our very traditions but gradually voters have forgotten how to question and change the status quo when the need is evident. We have not kept alive the spirit of creative inquiry and dissent passed on to us by our revolutionary generation.

> "They accomplished a revolution which has no parallel in the annals of human society. They reared the fabrics of government which have no model on the face of the globe. They formed the design of a great Confederacy, which it is incumbent on our successors to improve and perpetuate."[7]

> Alexander Hamilton

Given the failures of legislators in our present political environment, it is now incumbent upon the current generation of voters, the "successors" in our american experiment, to "improve and perpetuate" our system of representative government. We cannot simply blame our current morass on our forefathers lack of insight into human nature. Instead, we must make bold new provisions for protecting our republic from one of the worst of human political vices - desire for reelection.

Our first line of inquiry regarding the defects in our system of political representation should be why the framers thought it wise to employ the dubious process of reelection? Do we need multiple terms of office? And what useful purpose has reelection served? Can we say that the institution of reelection to date has served to police, or pervert, the political process?

It is my belief that reelection, in itself, in our time, is a mistake. It is both unnecessary and harmful to the interests of the body politic.

The basic idea proposed here is that we must now consider eliminating the process of re-election altogether. With longer single terms of office, thus removing the evils of incumbency and reelection, we can reinvigorate electoral politics. With longer single terms we will eliminate the greatest of modern obstacles to honest and effective government - reelection and its attendant frauds upon the people.

But before we consider the need for such reform we might well ask what it is that voters gain or lose with a political process that motivates our elected representatives to neglect their rightful duties and begin raising money from special-interests, literally from the very day they take office? The plain truth is that today we have too many representatives who, while ostensibly working for the taxpayers, are busy involved in their own career pursuits. This inherent conflict-of-interest, brought about by reelection, is a serious and continuing threat to good government.

With short terms of office, and re-election on the horizon, there is little doubt campaign fund-raising will be at the top of a representative's agenda. In fact, many legislators today are perpetually involved in the process of reelection and campaign fundraising. The cancer in our political system is that so many elected officials, and challengers, are desperate for campaign funds and thus perennially on the make.

The thesis of a one-term solution is that the process of frequent reelection, and largely unrestricted election campaign fundraising, combine today to form a lethal virus that eats away at the vitals of our republic. The antithesis is clear.

> "Whether we look at city councils, state legislatures or the Congress of the United States, we react to what we see with scarcely concealed contempt. This is the area where democratic government is breaking down. This is where vested-interest lobbies tend to run riot, where conflict of interest is concealed from the public ... I have no hesitation in stating my deep conviction that the legislatures of America, local, state and national, are presently the greatest menace in our country to the successful operation of the democratic process."[8]
>
> Sen. Joseph S. Clark

Many who have served in Congress, and state legislatures, readily agree with former Senator Clark. It appears we now have a system guaranteed to bring out the worst in political office holders. The pressures of ego-humiliation, not to mention the lose of power, status, and income resulting from a reelection defeat is precisely the situation creating the temptation to bend and bribe the system to the office-holder's personal advantage. The political process, as it now stands, slowly perverts even those with the best of intentions. Any idealism existing in our newly elected representatives soon dissipates as reelection time approaches.

The temptations of a political career are legion. And the results of our current system are now evident. Richard Goodwin, a political journalist, aptly defined the problem: "Our national legislative process has become corrupt. The money power is becoming the congressional power. This fact is now readily acknowledged, in private, even by those who are struggling to restore integrity and principle to democratic government. It has been a losing battle. And we, the governed, whose consent is no longer asked or needed, are the losers."

Can we do better? Can we expect more from our elected officials under the present system? It doesn't matter whether we are talking about our city councilpersons, mayors, state assemblymen, congressmen, senators, or a governor or president, the process is the same. Once elected, reelection becomes the common goal and the essential sub-rosa agenda of office holders. Regardless of the office the process is the same. And it is even more virulent and corrupt in the case of an incumbent's bid for reelection.

Can we assume the voting public will get the best possible representation under our present system? The answer is clearly not. But just what reforms would likely insure the voters have a real choice from amongst the best a community or nation has to offer? And once elected, to see to it that the interests of the public are not subordinated to the personal self-interests of the representative?

Are we attracting enough capable and qualified people to public office today? Are many of our most qualified citizens simply not "running" because of the very nature of the election system, with its demands for huge sums of money, media hype, and the subjection to largely inappropriate peeping-tom journalistic crusades into our private lives?

In short, what sort of a political system have we created, or better, allowed to flourish?

REELECTION - THE NEXUS POINT OF CORRUPTION

"All members of congress have a primary interest in being reelected... and some members have no other interest."[9]

Rep. Frank E. Smith

Any person desirous of maintaining the privileges of public office and career tenure will find ways to insure their survival. It can safely be said that our political problems don't stem from an underdose of intelligence or ability. Instead, they arise from intelligence perverted by the ego, by the facade, and the perceived needs of the persona. Yet good government demands near selfless representation in order to produce effective and proper decision-making for our communities and the nation. Is such selfless representation, free of conflicts-of-interest, wholly unrealistic? Or is it simply unlikely under our present system?

The self-preservation instinct, when applied to maintaining oneself in public office, is truly the nexus point of political corruption. For this reason reelection should be eliminated - reelection is the Achilles heel of the republic.

We don't need to psychoanalyze politicians, and our new candidates for office, as much as we need to effectively insulate them from confusing personal needs with public needs. Reelection is the point at which this confusion and conflict of loyalties becomes serious. Thus, it makes sense to eliminate reelection as often as possible in the interests of true representation and good government.

By eliminating reelection, and the on-going needs of the political-ego, we can protect the body politic from the serious distortion of the legislative process. At the same time we will attract more people of ability and virtue to public office who may be currently unwilling, or unable, to enter the arena. And since we cannot require that all political participants become saints, we can only restructure our system to eliminate, or substantially reduce, the long-term mischief potential.

Only with longer single terms can we reasonably expect to protect our representatives from the perils of the reelection syndrome. Single terms of office will more effectively insulate our elected officials from the illegitimate demands of election campaigns, the bribes of powerful special-interest groups and the candidate's own egocentric foibles. Otherwise, come reelection time, wisdom, fairness, and responsibility are almost certain to disappear in a sea of promises.

Rampant conflict-of-interest is destroying our prospects for good government. And it is the very process of reelection itself that forms the basis of our representative's inherent conflicts. Ralph Nader aptly summarized incumbents advantages:

> "With the power to supervise the laws governing his own reelection, with the power to make news, with the power to determine, in many cases, what kind of news about himself filters back to his district, with the power to cater to special interests and to accept their money, the incumbent also has enormous opportunities for corruption, for unfairness, for deceit and manipulation of the public. One of them is every single member of congress is a walking, talking embodiment of conflict-of-interest. On the one hand, he has an interest in staying in office, in being reelected; on the other, he has, or ought to have, an interest in serving his constituents and the nation honorably."[10]

To understand what political reforms may now be necessary to counter this systemic problem, we must inquire whether the framers could possibly have foreseen the day when legislators would be reelected so often, and incumbents would possess such overwhelming advantages and self-serving opportunities at public expense? It is certainly unlikely they could possibly have envisioned the sheer number, and monetary power, of our modern day special-interest groups? Two hundred year ago, few could have foreseen the scope of excesses prevalent in the political arena today, and fewer still could have imagined the power of the incumbent in our new age of hi-tech media machinery.

Why did our founding fathers consider reelection necessary?

Is reelection a political necessity, a god-given right, or ultimately a perversion of representative government?

What was the substance of the debate over terms of office and duty to the people at our first Constitutional Convention?

In short, why do we have the system we have?

And, most importantly, why is it so seldom examined for its efficacy?

Before we attempt to answer these questions we should reflect upon the fact the constitution was written at a time when representatives were known, and often personally encountered, by their constituents in the daily course of events. The world was a smaller place. The framers of the constitution were active and known in the local community and regularly seen at church. And from these coherent communities they were sent off on horseback, or carriage, to represent their constituency. At the time of the birth of our constitution the average american community was more intimate, involved, and in far better control of their nomination and election processes. The urban world of today, with our mind-bending technology and media influences, is fundamentally different from the eighteenth century political environment of our forefathers.

In recent times we have witnessed a significant shift in the balance of power between voters and their representatives. Today, legislators effectively manipulate "their" constituencies with a professional expertise and technological power unknown in earlier years.

Has technology proceeded to shred the intent of certain provisions of our constitution? Or, in the alternative, at some time in the near future will democracy possibly be re-vitalized by our media? The answer remains unclear.

James Madison once observed that the "natural limit of a democracy is that distance from the central point which will just permit the most remote citizens to assemble as often as their public function demands, and will include no greater number than can join in those functions." Thus the absolute size of political assemblies was an important question in designing proper representation. At the time of our confederation it was estimated that one congressional representative would serve no more than thirty thousand people at most. Today, however, each representative, on average, serves over five hundred thousand people, and often in blissful anonymity.

In this respect, perhaps the limits of representation have been greatly exceeded. And voters punching computerized ballots for names of candidates, either totally unfamiliar or vaguely recognized from bumper stickers and television commercials, constitutes a process that does not compare with the physical and intimate political participation of yesteryear. Ironically, our increased communication power seems to have resulted in bringing about less participation in community affairs and not more. Over time we have moved well beyond the "natural limits" of democracy - and therein lies our problem.

A POLITICAL TRAP?—

> "And if he should be desirous of being continued, his wishes, conspiring with his fears, would tend still more powerfully to corrupt his integrity, or debase his fortitude."[11]

Alexander Hamilton

Hamilton, among others at the convention, well understood the magnetic pull of power and political office as well as the potentially destructive force of desire for reelection. And with regard to duration in office and the "energy" of the president, he pondered over the problem of desire and ambition, and the ultimate confusion of public duty with private interests. He knew the body politic is often beset by "the wiles of parasites and sycophants, by the snares of the ambitious, the avaricious, the desperate, by the artifices of men who possess their confidence more than deserve it, and of those who seek to possess rather than deserve it."[12]

This is precisely our problem today. We are now beset by political figures who want to possess the office rather than deserve it. And it is precisely the "runners" from whom we must protect ourselves.

However, to date we have no provisions for appointing, as opposed to electing, our political representatives on a merit basis. Rather we "elect" a largely self-appointed "candidate" from amongst those who "run" for office, after they have raised sufficient funds from special-interests to enter the "race." In this type of spurious "nomination" process merit seldom enters the equation. Many would agree with the proposition that we are getting the government we deserve due to the nature of the system we continue to employ.

For the most part, however, we have not yet experienced a government where individuals of merit are selected, recommended, appointed, and then "elected" to represent the interests of the people. Instead, we must beat back the crowd of office seekers whose political qualifications and personal agendas are suspect. We have severely limited our field of potential candidates to those who "want" and covet the office, as if this were a criteria of acceptability for enormous political responsibility.

In fact, we could hardly design a worse system of political representation than what we exist with today. Why, we might ask, should we preserve an electoral system, developed two hundred years ago, for a world that no longer exists? Would the framers respect our political acumen for allowing the present political order to continue? The answer is clearly not.

We must simply eliminate, or at least greatly diminish, the obvious conflicts-of-interest built into such a system. But it is our very worship of the constitution and our sundry political traditions that could prove to be a major problem. The prospect of change, of amending our constitution, is so frightening to some people that even given better alternatives they might never overcome their fears. However, progress in government, and human relations, necessitates a cold look at reality.

The inertia of a long political tradition is a tough force to overcome. But to examine the current reality of our political institutions is to overcome the sleep of tradition and sheer force of our conservative partiotic instincts that so effectively prevents experimentation and change. However, once the necessity for reform, and viable options, are more fully understood by the voting public the force of change will be nearly impossible to stop. And change we must.

"I like a little rebellion now and then. The spirit of resistance to government is so valuable on occasion that I wish it to be always kept alive."[13]

Benjamin Franklin

The calm and unruffled demeanor of Benjamin Franklin hardly concealed the rebellious spirit, wit, and intelligence of "the good doctor." He, like others amongst our original rebels, well understood the need for periodic political change and thus acted to solve the problems of their own time and circumstance. There is little question electoral politics has degenerated from the lofty plateaus envisioned by the framers and that change is once again imperative. Today, in turn, we must act boldly to improve and enliven our system of political representation.

Longer single terms of representation can, I believe, go a long way toward solving the current problem of too short two-year congressional terms that lead to full time fund-raising and tend to give special interests, and not the people, a stranglehold on their representatives. In the same fashion, at the presidential level, four-year terms become effectively three due to delays and inaction during reelection years.

Despite short terms the average representative is nearly invisible to voters but certainly not to special-interests. The fact is special-interest groups know who their congressman is and how they have voted on critical issues. However, we cannot say the same for the average voter. In this regard, Nader also observed: "It would seem to the uninitiated that the need to seek frequent reelection would make congressman listen more closely to the opinions of their constituents. Instead, because the costs of campaigning are so high, the perennial campaign makes congressman listen more closely to their campaign contributors."[14]

This simple fact of political life is reiterated by many candidates caught in a trap and an election system they neither like nor seem to be able to change. And the trap has its price. Senator Thomas Eagleton stated: "I would say that an incumbent senator in a hotly contested reelection campaign

20

would devote seventy to eighty percent of his personal time, effort, thought, and worrying to fund-raising for the last two years of a six-year term."[15] Representative Michael Barnes echoed his concerns: "As I spoke to political consultants, they all said I should not even consider running for the Senate if I weren't prepared to spend 80 or 90 percent of my time raising money."[16]

Of what value is today's process of "perennial electioning" by politicians eager to hold onto the perquisites of power? The reelection syndrome has undermined the very nobility of our great institutions. Our representatives are forced into seriously compromised positions, and our political future is held hostage to major campaign contributors with a hammerlock on politicians who cannot stand the thought of serving only one term in office!

Single terms, or at the very least longer and fewer terms, in addition to further campaign finance reform, would greatly diminish, if not altogether eliminate, our representative's serious conflict-of-interests arising from the seeking, and acceptance, of campaign funds from lobbys seeking to influence pending legislation. The reality is such that a simple hint of adverse legislation, from powerful Senate and House committee chairmen, can unleash a torrent of political "contributions" more appropriately described as bribes.

It can safely be said that power, and reelection campaign financing, corrupt absolutely.

POLITICS AS A CAREER?—

For our inquiry to succeed we must ask what type of person is attracted to public life and a political career under our current system? Is service the predominating motive? And once in office, are candidates simply perpetuating at public expense what was once a legitimate short-term aspiration?

Should it be possible to make politics a lifetime career? Do we need, or can we afford, career politicians? What are the risks or benefits, if any, of depending upon career politicians to protect the vital interests of the body politic?

21

The benefits of lifetime political employment are certainly not clear. In fact, excessive length in any one position of office, be it public or private, may simply corrode, pervert, and dim our vision and understanding of issues. Perception of the necessary and the possible may be dulled by years of compromise suffused with personal interest. For this reason generations of career politicians, on both sides of the political fence, have been more adept at perpetuating differences than dissolving them.

How then do we arrange our system of representation, and elections, to attract people of merit filled with ideals of service to their community and nation, a spirit of independence, and not a whit's concern about reelection, power or influence? Do such individuals exist? Or does our system, as it exists, simply attract the careerist mentality and then entrap and further corrupt them? And does the present multi-term system also repel many meritorious candidates today? A good case can be made for this latter theory. A central problem is that people of merit interested in a single-term of public service in their city, state, or nation, are up against hard-core careerists and power brokers for whom the word "service" has lost all meaning. Tragically, politics, as it stands today, is a world too many able people wish to avoid... and some might say with good reason.

Sadly, it is now mostly those seeking the intrigue of the political game who will be moved to enter a campaign. Mavericks and uncommitted individuals unwilling to meet the standards of special-interest group financiers need not apply. As a result, ideals and real debate have largely vanished from politics - only money and soporific slogans remain.

It is a recurring spectacle today to see our politicians congratulating themselves on their continuing reelection, rather than real accomplishments or vigor in pursuing less-than-popular issues. Reelection has thus become a virtue unto itself.

The truth is our american spirit of political revolution and independence is not yet dead although it may well appear to be buried. A new second awakening, a second revolution, is now stirring. Regarding the political nature of our early colonists and perhaps of our buried instincts as well, De Tocqueville, in 1835, wrote about our peculiar yankee character in the classic Democracy in America. He noted citizens of the colonies were passionate political participants eager to prevent usurptation of their rights by ambitious careerists:

> "The township of New England is so constituted as to excite the warmest of human affections, without arousing the ambitious passions of the heart of man. The officers of the county are not elected, and their authority is very limited. Even the state is only a second-rate community whose tranquil and obscure administration offers no inducement sufficient to draw men away from the home of their interests into the turmoil of public affairs. The native of New England is attached to his township because it is independent and free; this cooperation in its affairs insures his attachment to its interest; the well-being it affords him secures his affection; and its welfare is the aim of his ambition and of his future exertions. He takes a part in every occurrence in the place; he practises the art of government in the small sphere within his reach."[17]

Originally, as De Toqueville indicates, many municipal officials were appointed rather than elected. Early americans had no truck with ambitious braggarts attempting to carve out a cozy life at community expense. Appointments were preferred because they knew that elections often brought out the worst in men and, consequently, in government.

However, unlike the New England environment of yesteryear, the majority of citizens today live in large urban and suburban environments. With the average family moving every few years, often transferred by large organizations for purely economic reasons, leading to a more nomadic life style in general, neither representative nor constituent may be in one place very long. Due to increasing urbanization, most representatives no longer have a single small town constituency - thus politics is now big business in more ways than one.

As a result of societal changes, voters have lost much of this sense of community. We have become a "global village" without attachment to any village we can call our own. We are hard pressed to identify the logical extent or boundaries of our community? As a result, many voters today cannot name, or even recognize, their local officials, congressmen, or senators.

Further evidence of our political decline is provided by the fact that most constituencies today are just blocks of unrelated and gerrymandered suburbs thrown together to make a "district." The very word denotes, not a viable community or a cohesive human place, but an arbitrary space thrown together by a computer feeding on census statistics.

The increasingly transient nature of American society makes it ever more difficult for people to involve themselves in local affairs, and even to get registered to vote. Beleaguered with the daily problems of making a living, hours spent commuting, and attempting to have a family life, there is too little time or energy left for many people to inquire about what is happening in their community. In this continuing political vacuum, incumbency will thrive.

Without revolving citizen participation in civic affairs, aided by such innovations as single-term initiatives, it appears certain our legions of career politicians and bureaucrats will ultimately assume all power and influence. Where longevity in office and civil service is the prevailing game and guiding rule, the majority of citizens will soon be powerless against the might of the bureaucratic and corporate state.

We are not alone, however, in attempting to tame monolithic political forces. Consider the dilemma of the Russian people and Premier Gorbachev's courageous fight to trim the mammoth Soviet bureaucracy. A central tenet of his "Perestroika" reform program is the need to limit the terms of party members serving in the politburo and other agencies. Initially, a limit of two terms has been proposed to combat

24

the utter stagnation brought about by rubber-stamp reelections and lifetime appointments of career party officials.

One might speculate that if special-interest groups ever acquire the same power and status in the Soviet Union they have managed to achieve in the United States, it is likely the Russian people also will move toward a single-term solution to avoid the reelection/corruption process. No more career party officials - this is the essence of Perestroika. The Russian people have seen the light, or should we say, the darkness.

An American "Perestroika" will be a one-term revolution.

WHAT'S SO SACRED ABOUT A TWO-YEAR TERM?

"I will ask you to make it possible for members of the House of Representatives to work more effectively in the service of the nation through a constitutional amendment extending the term of a congressman concurrent with that of a president... The two-year term requires most members of congress to divert enormous energies to an almost constant process of campaigning, depriving this nation of the fullest measure of both their skill and their wisdom. Today, too, the work of government is far more complex than in our early years, requiring more time to learn and more time to master the technical tasks of legislating. And a longer term will serve to attract more men of the highest quality to political life."[18]

President Lyndon Johnson

Changing the term of office for President, Senators, and Representatives has been discussed many times in the history of our republic. In 1966, President Johnson prescribed just such a change in congressional and presidential terms to protect the nation from the evils of reelection and short terms of office. After a long career in Congress Lyndon Johnson was well aware there was a better way. Unfortunately, he waited until he was safely ensconced in the presidency to make the suggestion that this fundamental change was absolutely necessary. But he understood Congress would not likely make such a change in their own affairs. The only possible route for reform was to be via a constitutional amendment - the people have to legislate.

The principle of accountability to one's constituents, that underlay the principle of frequent elections, has been perverted by time and circumstance. The very rational behind the idea of the lower house, a House of Representatives, is that it would become a vital and tumultuous political body alive with constant change and periodic transfusions of new blood. In theory, short congressional terms of office and frequent turnover were deemed necessary to keep representatives tied to their constituents while balancing the longer run continuity of the Senate with its six-year terms and aristocratic tendencies.

However, as former Representative Clem Long observed, the rational of a short term for congressional representatives is an idea whose time has come and gone: "It was instituted at a time when the average congressman represented only a few thousand instead of hundreds of thousands of constituents; when congress met a month or two instead of nearly all year; and when the federal government confined its activities to national defense, the excise tax, and a few internal improvements, instead of pervading every aspect of personal and business life and spending a quarter to a third of all the income of the economy."[19]

In other words, the present congressional term is not long enough to do justice to the job. And to compound the problem, just as a representative gets grounded in the job it is time to start thinking about reelection. Congressmen must now face reelection every two years and, as a result, campaigning never ends. Their energies are constantly diverted from the task at hand. A representative's inclination for self-preservation soon begins to override their allegiance to the people of their district and the nation.

Lately, more political observers have come to realize the wisdom of Lyndon Johnson's recommendations. Under our present system we paralyze our legislators with the physical, financial, and ethically mind-bending demands of reelection. At the same time we cripple any hope of solutions to our most pressing problems requiring any degree of political fortitude. With a multi-term perspective, reelection on the horizon and campaign expenses to raise, representatives are overwhelmed. The voting public today does not get their money's worth of representation.

With shorter terms and frequent elections, the framers believed voters would have a good handle on any misfeasance by their representatives. Run up a deficit, debase the currency, or crank up imperial war machines in defiance of the public will and, it was assumed, they would soon be retired. And given the power of the purse, it was originally intended that Congress was not to be too remote from the people's swift revenge. Perhaps this arrangement looked good on paper, but our modern reality has proved to be another matter.

Interestingly enough the idea of limiting terms goes back as far as the first Continental Congress in 1777, where under the Articles of Confederation, the delegates were limited to only three years service in any six-year period. A decade later, at the Constitutional Convention in 1787, limits were debated but not set. And when we examine the framers original debate, there was clearly no consensus for a two-year congressional term. What resulted was simply no more than a compromise between proposals for a one-year and a three-year term - nothing magic or sacred about it.

On the one hand, Samuel Adams contended that "where annual elections end, tyranny begins."[20] But Madison argued for a three-year term favoring stability: "three years will be necessary, in a government so extensive, for members to form any knowledge of the various interests of the states to which they do not belong, and of which they can know but little from the situation and affairs of their own."[21] Today, this same longer term logic would suggest a four, or even six-year, congressional term. Perhaps a one or two-year term suited the needs of the Colonists two centuries ago. However, we can now argue, as have Lyndon Johnson and others, that we need to give legislators more time to execute faithfully the duties of their position. But along with a longer single term there should be no more time, in the form of additional terms, to cave in to the temptation to sell one's vote and gain anything beyond the term of that office.

A majority of our original colonists, rightfully suspicious of any governing body beyond the town council, wanted quick and easy control over their representatives and viewed anything but annual elections as a "prelude to tyranny." They may well have solved their problem and created ours. For they could not foresee our modern problems with the sheer power of incumbency nullifying the supposedly curative effect of frequent elections.

WHY NOT A LONGER SINGLE TERM? —

"Clearly, too, the men who framed the constitution expected that congressmen would not get reelected as regularly as they are now; that is the whole argument behind the two-year term for members of the House of Representatives. The Senate would represent continuity, and the House change... Ironically, in a mass society, where each member has about half a million constituents, the two-year term has come to accomplish exactly the opposite of its purpose. It was supposed to give the people a chance to hold their representatives accountable every two years. Now, however, the two-year term has given special interests a chance to hold their representatives accountable every two years."[22]

Ralph Nader

The original rational for the length of any political term was obviously related to the needs and duties of the office in question. A bicameral legislative approach and a working

28

system of checks and balances required, in theory, a combination of short and long terms.

For this reason it was contemplated by the framers that congressional terms of 1-3 years would be appropriate to maintain the people's frequent access to censure of their representatives. On the other hand, the senate terms proposed ranged from three, four, five, six, seven, and nine-year terms to "during good behavior." It was generally believed the Senate, with fewer members and longer terms, would exert a stabilizing influence over a group of unruly populist congressmen with uncertain and, for the time, all too democratic agendas. A seven-year senate term was accepted and voted by the constitutional committee with an eight to one margin, only to be changed the next day to a six-year term with "one-third of the members to go out every second year."[23]

Clearly there was disagreement on the appropriate length of both congressional and senatorial terms. For this reason alone we should not view the current terms today as somehow inviolable. The framers debate and eventual compromise indicates the two-year congressional and six-year senate terms were simply the only compromise possible amidst a wide variety of opinions. Present terms of office locked into our constitution are not the result of divine inspiration but simply the sum of political compromise. Consequently, one is hard pressed to claim these compromises somehow constitute optimum terms of office.

The essence of this compromise position on long vs. short terms of office was aptly stated by Fisher Ames, a Massachusetts delegate at the convention: "The term of office must be so long, that the representative may understand the interest of the people, and yet so limited, that his fidelity may be secured by a dependence upon their approbation."[24] So long, and yet so limited, indeed.

Madison and Hamilton even favored life terms for senators, fearing the populist sentiments of a congress with egalitarian tendencies. Ironically, however, life terms are exactly what many incumbents in the Congress and Senate are able to manage today given their tremendous advantages and manipulative power over challengers.

Charles O. Jones stressed another important rationale in this compromise: "the existence of shorter terms and popular election for House members, it seems, permitted the creation of an aristocratic senate."[25] Thus, a two-year house term, and the six-year senate term, emerged as what then seemed to be the best compromise given the nature and function of each body. It also represented, in another sense, the more marked class divisions of the day inherited from the mother country. And it was widely believed Congress would represent a "leveling spirit" given that it would consist largely of an unruly and contentious body of "freemen" from the hinterlands who lacked the wealth and social status of senate members. A majority of the framers may also have felt that short congressional terms would keep the rural populist troublemakers revolving out of power and out of the way of the aristocratic senate. Clearly, there is no reason not to view the framers as pragmatists as well as idealists.

In other words, the explicit rationale outlined in the Federalist Papers may not give us the complete picture of the debate over terms of office. And with the passage of time it is ever more difficult to pinpoint the unstated motivations behind the shaping of our political institutions. It may be that some of our slave-owning and hemp-growing ancestors were political sages, but they weren't necessarily saints. And it is also true that there were some nervous plantation owners at the convention who feared what a rag-tag body of lower house representatives might do if not reigned in by a strong senate.

Clearly, we cannot comprehend our political institutions without a better understanding of life in eighteenth-century America. Speaking of the "lower House," Jefferson remarked that "the tyranny of the legislature is really the danger most to be feared."[26] Today, while we appreciate his remark in one context we may not fully understand it in the context of his time. But one thing is certain, it can be safely said that the tyranny of any legislature is compounded by the modern tyranny of prolonged incumbency.

One may question whether a continuing "dependence" upon the voter's approval is now necessary, or beneficial, *after* one takes office. Certainly before one is elected there is a dependence and a seeking of approbation and approval via the vote. But once elected, a representative must be independent and free of further "approbation." Otherwise, the catering instinct is given new life and power. Of what value is a "representative" who may be dependent on special-interest financing to continue their hold on elective office? "Approbation" at the ballot box is now bought and conjured up by media specialists.

The question for our time is "fidelity" in office to whom? And for what? Are representatives bound to pursue their native parochial interests to the extent that our national interests collapse in ongoing impasse? Are senators from small states, representing a minority of the population, meant to be able to frustrate the will of the majority? Do shorter congressional terms bind the House members to local concerns to the extent that societal dysfunction occurs in a wild clash of special and regional interests? Who cleans up after congress? As one wag quipped, "Con-gress is the opposite of Pro-gress."[27]

Perfection of our political institutions will not, and did not, take place overnight. Good government is formed gradually - by trial and error. Soon voters will be moved to further refine and perfect our republic. The truth is that our constitution is a document-in-progress. It is not written on stone tablets, although divine authority is sometimes claimed. And no one can presume the constitution is ever finished. But refinement will never take place unless we are willing to experiment with, and improve, our government institutions.

Certainly our political traditions are not meant to have a stranglehold on the future? If we are truly free agents and masters of our own constitution, then consideration of changes in our system, via constitutional amendment, should not be viewed with alarm and disdain. We simply need to revise the terms of political office to free our representatives to deliver better government.

In this vein, Hamilton's comments about the president's term are applicable to our modern debate about eliminating reelection and lengthening terms of office:

> "It cannot be affirmed that a duration of four years, or any other limited duration, would completely answer the end proposed; but it would contribute towards it in a degree which would have a material influence upon the spirit and character of the government. Between the commencement and termination of such a period there would always be a considerable interval in which the prospect of annilihation (losing an election) would be sufficiently remote not to have an improper effect upon the conduct of a man endowed with a tolerable portion of fortitude; and in which he might reasonably promise himself that there would be time enough before it arrived to make the community sensible to the propriety of the measures he might incline to pursue. Though it be probable that, as he approached the moment when the public were, by a new election, to signify their sense of his conduct, his confidence, and with it his firmness, would decline."[28]

Hamilton recognized that elections, per se, interfere with representation - the less the better. "Confidence and firmness" in our representatives is thus much more likely to occur in the absence of reelection pressures.

Ours is a new age. And while the principles underlying the constitution may hold over time the practices may not. Are we then to squeeze the political realities of the twentieth century into the eighteenth? I don't think so. It was clearly not the intent of the framers of our constitution to create a document that would prohibit future inhabitants of our nation, in perpetuity, from similar experimentation to achieve superior government. They were dead set against dictatorship, be it of man or document.

TERM OF OFFICE - THE CONSTITUTIONAL DEBATE

> "A man acting in the capacity of chief magistrate, under a consciousness that in a very short time he must lay down his office, will be apt to feel himself too little interested in it to hazard any material censure or perplexity, from the independent exertion of his powers, or from encountering the ill-humors, however transient, which may happen to prevail. And if he should be desirous of being continued, his wishes, conspiring with his fears, would tend still more powerfully to corrupt his integrity, or debase his fortitude. In either case, feebleness and irresolution must be the characteristic of the station."[29]

Alexander Hamilton

"Feebleness and irresolution" characterizes politicians today constantly looking toward reelection. And the qualities of political firmness and independence are nearly immobilized by the vagaries of the short term. But even though Hamilton is speaking here of the presidential term, the dynamics are the same regardless of the post involved, and perhaps even more pernicious at the level of Representative.

This corrupting influence of "desire" for political office, and reelection, certainly did not escape deliberation by the framers. Hamilton was inclined to believe that there must be a "hope of obtaining" furtherance in office, and that a "desire of reward" is a stong motivator of human conduct and would somehow result in a magic exclusion of self-interests from performance of duty. Today, however, I think many would contend that it is precisely these egocentric concerns of "hope" and desire" that are the problem and not the solution.

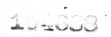

We have only to ask what the personal "hope and desire" of a politician seeking reelection contributes to national or local concerns? The fact is it simply interjects the concerns of the individual into important matters of state. How can we have good government when matters of self-interest intermingle, or prevail, over substantive issues? This is precisely our problem today - the hope and desire for reelection does not serve the interests of the voter nor exert any magic ethical influence upon the office-holder. The truth is that the influence of the reelection syndrome upon our government is clearly pernicious.

Hamilton understood well the dangers of short terms and the corrupting influence of a strong desire for reelection. But his inclination for two four-year executive terms was based on his preference for some form of "approbation" and ability to continue in office given the mandate of the people. His remarks, however, are even more applicable to our case for a one-term solution and a change to a single six-year presidential term and four-year congressional terms. If Hamilton sensed that, as reelection time approached, legislators would likely lose their firmness he then implicitly recognized the basic underlying problem - reelection and prolonged incumbency.

We might speculate as to whether the framers, with our greater appreciation of the effects of two hundred years worth of reelection fever upon our government, could not have come to different conclusions about appropriate terms of office. In their day the framers did not believe centuries old political arrangements were particularly suitable for thirteen rebellious colonial states. They wrote, for their own times, a document addressing the nature of their problems. And while human nature has not changed over the years, certainly the scope and power of the special-interests and media today are well beyond anything the framers of our constitution could foresee, envision, or even comprehend.

The framers believed the selection of an optimum term of office required a balance between independence and stability. In the Federalist papers Madison observed: "the genius of

34

republican liberty seems to demand on one side not only that all power should be derived from the people, but that those entrusted with it should be kept in dependence on the people by a short duration of their appointments. Stability, on the contrary, requires that the hands in which power is lodged should continue for a length of time the same."[30]

Our central problem today is that politicians are no longer "dependent" on the people. They are principally dependent on money to finance their campaigns. Votes are secondary, and more easily acquired after campaign financing has been arranged. When ambitious and career-oriented office holders are faced with meeting reelection demands, at what point in a two-year term can we say that confidence, firmness, and independence prevail? The precious qualities of "firmness" and "confidence" are even more necessary for legislators today who are called upon to achieve a just balance between the legitimate grievances and interests of diverse groups in our pluralistic society. Balancing the federal budget alone will require legislators to possess nerves of steel and harbor no further designs on political office. The task of taking the bacon away is going to be a lot harder job than bringing it home.

Thus, a more modern political "genius" will contemplate terms of office that better attain this balance of duration, stability, and continuity while dismantling the disadvantages of acquired power and conflict-of-interest. Longer single terms of political employment may well achieve this balance in better proportion than we have today. The corrupting process of frequent reelection has not served us well. We must now amend our blessed charter to combat the evils of our own time.

OBJECTIONS TO THE SINGLE TERM —

> "Nothing appears more plausible at first sight, nor more ill-founded upon close inspection, than a scheme which in relation to the present point has had some respectable advocates, I mean that of continuing the chief magistrate in office for a

certain time, and then excluding him from it, either
for a limited period or forever after."[31]

Alexander Hamilton

The idea of a single term, both for the president and
our representatives, was not without its detractors at our first
Constitutional Convention. It was Alexander Hamilton who
seemed to have the most reservations about such a limitation.

One of Hamilton's principal objections to the single term
relates to his belief that there would be a "diminuition of the
inducements to good behavior." The implicit assumption here
is that the spectre of reward, in the form of reelection, somehow
causes "good" as opposed to corrupted behavior. The opposite
seems to be the case however. This very debatable proposition
appears especially naive given the present day antics of poll-
watching office holders and what they will, or won't, do to
insure their reelection?

It is important to remember that a single-term limitation
is not meant to be political punishment, but simply a device
thru which the electorate can protect themselves from self-
serving representatives. If we begin with the premise that
somehow one must be "rewarded" in order to enter, or remain,
in public life then, in that event, we should leave it alone.

Another of Hamilton's reservations about single terms
had to do with the perennial problem of opportunity and
opportunists: "An avaricious man, who might happen to fill
the office, looking forward to a time when he must at all events
yield up the emoluments he enjoyed, would feel a propensity,
not easy to be resisted by such a man, to make the best use
of the opportunity he enjoyed while it lasted and might not
scruple to have recourse to the most corrupt expedients to
make the harvest as abundant as it was transitory."[32]

This objection, however, applies to temptations at the
end of any term whether we speak of one term or ten. In
this sense it does not directly impact the proposal for single
terms. And, regardless, the problem of "Integrity in Post-
Employment" and the temptation to personally profit upon

exiting from public office will always be with us regardless of the number or length of terms in office. A strengthening of Post-Employment laws will help in this regard.

But does the process of reelection somehow transform our representatives and induce "good" behavior? Or does it simply add to the pressures and temptations of candidates to promise something to every conceivable constituency, while at the same time, avoiding necessary actions that may offend any particular group? Does it not interfere with good government?

On the other hand, will a single term setup attract more corrupt men or more noble men? Will the ethical standards of the majority of candidates be any different than they are now? Will government improve? We will never know the answers to these questions until we explore alternatives to our present system. I believe we have little to lose and much to gain from single-term reforms.

Another one of Hamilton's objections to "exclusion" from additional terms of office had to do with the basic question of experience.[33] By eliminating reelection, are we depriving the community of good judgment and other benefits gained from experience in office? One can make a case for this argument but it would imply that "experience" in one's life and profession, before holding office, have little or no value. Today, this argument, as we will see in Chapter V, is largely invalidated by the reality of the information revolution.

Can we then accept the implication here that newly elected single-term representatives would somehow be tabula rasa upon entering the legislative chamber? Is political judgment better in the first, or fifteenth year, of office? And does not fifteen or even thirty years of political office, as is the case with many jobs, merely translate into one year's experience repeated over and over? Under a continuous relection system might we not say that a representative's behavior may, after numerous terms, simply be less idealistic and tending to be perverted by the self-preservation cancer?

37

In other words, can we accept the common argument that the judgment, knowledge, or experience, of one who has been in office more years than another is of more value per se? Clearly, unless we examine a specific issue, and a specific legislator, we cannot make such a judgment. Generalizations on the issue of political experience serve to promote incumbency and deny the vitality of new blood and fresh approaches.

Hamilton's fourth "ill effect" of limiting terms of office revolved around the idea that certain emergencies of state would "necessitate" the continuing of the incumbent at a crucial time.

He felt that "a change of the chief magistrate, at the outbreak of a war or any similar crisis, for another, even of equal merit, would at all times be detrimental to the community, inasmuch as it would substitute inexperience to experience, and would tend to unhinge and set afloat the already settled train of the administration."[34] In effect, however, this idea simply mandates the personality cult, the fourth Roosevelt term, and the megalomania of the careerist politician.

Certainly there is transition time in any change of office, regardless of whether it occurs after four, six, or even eight years. Transitions must occur, otherwise we have dictatorship. But here too we might also argue that continuous reelection, given the current advantages of the incumbent, is a new and subtle form of political dictatorship.

This fourth argument of Hamilton strikes me as the weakest of his objections to a single term. Certainly there have been traumatic times in our history, such as the assasination of four presidents, when uncertainty was introduced into our affairs. Confusion and uncertainty can occur despite the fact that we have vice-presidents and a clear chain of succession. But whether the change is by election, assasination, death in office, or other incapacitating circumstances, transition in emergencies is well provided for. The illusory identification of a nation's welfare with a specific person, and that office holder's tendency to be overly concerned with "their place in history" is a dangerous situation. The very sickness of political power tends to raise its ugly head at these critical junctures, namely reelection.

There have been many instances throughout history where the real truth has been that dictators, presidents, and emperors have incited or manufactured crisis, at critical junctures, for the express purpose of holding onto their power. The annals of history are filled with political Ayatollahs who, when power was due to be transferred, moved to eliminate their opposition and construct divinely inspired scenarios of "manifest destiny" to justify war and oppression and divert attention from domestic failures. The lessons of history teach us that the longer one serves in office the more dangerous this ego-maniacal tendency becomes.

In retrospect, a one-term ethic could have saved many countries from tyranny and prevented bloodshed in innumerable circumstances. When reelection approaches all manner of mischief may be created by incumbents to guarantee continuance in office. But such temptations to perpetuate residency in office should not be built *into* a system - rather they should be removed.

The fact that a one-term solution may cut short the career of a good legislator is of less importance than the fact that it will also shorten the careers of the ineffectual, the unethical, the irresponsible, and the dangerous. The benefits appear to outweigh any possible disadvantages.

Hamilton's fifth "ill effect" of exclusion, from more than one term of office, is based on the assumption that it would "operate as a constitutional interdiction of stability in the administration."[35] Here, he implicitly recognizes the instability created by the reelection process itself. However, with a single six-year presidential term, for example, this would not be the case any more than the transition after two four-year terms. And how would the "ill effect" of "exclusion" contribute more to instability in the former case and not the latter?

In fact we have had relative "stability" for two hundred years, not because of multiple terms of office but often in spite of it. With elections for Congress every two years, how can this necessity possibly promote the stability of their function? And would not stability be increased by lengthening the term to four years, and the presidential term to 6 years? Perhaps the real stability we seek will also come from attracting and electing to office more stable people, shorn of desire for long-term elective office?

Regardless, the hope and desire of the electorate is simply that we will attract able men and women without self-serving and corrupting long-term political career aspirations. Voters must hope that more persons of merit will find it appealing to carve out a period of years in their life when they feel obligated to return something to the system which has given them liberty and, perhaps, fortune.

Lastly, Hamilton suggested that "there is a excess of refinement in the idea of disabling the people to continue in office men who had entitled themselves, in their opinion, to approbation and confidence; the advantages of which are at best speculative and equivocal, and are overbalanced by disadvantages far more certain and decisive."[36] Today, the disadvantages of frequent reelection are far more evident than they were in Hamilton's time. And the advantages of single terms may not be so speculative or equivocal. Perhaps our system of government needs a little "excess refinement." After all, as Madison stated: "If men were Angels, no government would be necessary."[37]

Despite the seemingly salutary premise of multiple terms, modern electorates have now seen the effects of "hope and desire" for reelection upon generations of politicians unable to separate self-interest from the genuine interests of the electorate. And there is no denying voters are now paying for the effects of this reelection syndrome.

LENGTHENING TERMS OF OFFICE —

"One of the problems we have is too many elections.
That is one of the advantages of the six-year term.
We would increase the House term to three years.

I suggest that the people elected to the Senate
very often intend to spend their entire lives there.
They come for thirty-five or forty years. They are
babes in arms when they come because they have
never done anything except run for office. I would
like to see more people in Congress who had done
something else."[38]

Charles Bartlett

Implicit in a one-term approach is a lengthening of the
basic term of office. A better approach would be to extend
the presidential term to six years and congressional terms to
a minimum of four years. The "stability and firmness" sought
by the framers would be enhanced by such an approach. And
the elimination of continuing incumbency would open the door
to many more deserving candidates.

It is not enough to criticize the current abuses of elective
political office without imagining the potential for similar abuse
in any alternative system. Can we then weigh, in advance, the
merits and disadvantages and perhaps emerge with a
satisfactory understanding of what a one-term approach would
likely accomplish? Will we simply have political candidates
leapfrogging from one office to another? Will representatives
just get good and then leave office? Will attachment to political
and media fame corrupt even single-term representatives into
continuing a public career at any expense? Will a one-term
approach amount to a "revolving door" government that simply
elevates the power of the civil service and bureaucracy?

These are important questions. But will the potential
disadvantages of single terms somehow outweigh the benefits?
I don't believe so.

Lengthening the term of office certainly does not remove
the constitutional protections of mid-term impeachment or
recall. In fact, it may well enliven these civic remedies if the
body politic sours on an elected official early in the term. Today,
these remedies are seldom used except in the most eggregious
cases of abuse, and usually only after court indictments and
trials have clearly established guilt. However, the utilization

41

of impeachment and recall should not be so cumbersome for the people that they remain a remote possibility in the mind of the errant politician.

What are the possible negatives, if any, of single-term service in government? We must understand that one-term service may simply mean a single term in a particular office. It does not need to imply that one should only hold one office in his or her lifetime. It does not mean that a popular and successful governor or senator cannot run for president - this would be a natural step. A one-term solution means only that the individual cannot be allowed to achieve a hegemony over the office, thru the power of incumbency, leading to a virtual certainty of reelection.

With a successful six-year term as a senator or governor behind an individual, for example, they would now be more publicly visible and eligible for a presidential bid. But that is not to say that only elected office holders will ever run for office. There is simply no reason why political parties must continue to nominate only existing office holders, or even why candidates must belong to a party. This is a large part of our problem - politicians breed politicians.

There is little question our next crop of legislators will face unprecedented budget and finance problems resulting from the irresponsibility of previous generations of politicians. Our future economic options may very well be limited. "Inflate or Die" is how one economist described our current financial dilemma. We must count on our representatives to keep our fiscal house in order. But these same fiscal decisions have become political dynamite too easily avoided and passed to future generations of taxpayers while incumbents evade their proper responsibility. This continuing intransigence can be attributed solely to the reelection process.

We have only to look to former members of Congress, now removed from the reelection game, to get the truth about our legislators. The comments of former Representative, Thomas F. Hartnett, are particularly revealing:

"Consider my experience. I was elected in November 1980, one of 54 Republicans... and I had never met a brighter, more enthusiastic and determined group than that class. We seemed united in our desire to bring about fiscal responsibility, conservative government and common sense - to make changes in the direction of this country. And we did, for about six months. Then our thoughts turned to the reelection that faced all of us. Who among us would want to go home having voted for cuts in veterans benefits, medicare, farm subsidies, student loans, or Social Security? No one. Who wants to be cut up by an opponent the next time around, when going along on all the various spending measures can ensure a long tenure in office? Fiscal responsibility goes out the window... We no longer have government of, by, and for the people, but rather by professional legislators who, using the perks of office, are re-elected time and again to the House and Senate."[39]

Unless we reform our system, the reelection syndrome will be our undoing. Not only do our legislators spend us into debt but they also avoid decisions on crucial issues. Our politicians don't decide - and that is the decision! Evasion of "hot" issues is the politically pragmatic "solution." And when there is a failure of collective political will amongst our legislators the prevailing practice is to delay action, study the issue for decades, and eventually pass the problem onto the next generation of legislators. Increasingly, this is the fate of many issues where potential solutions step on special-interest toes and threaten re-electable politicians so hungry for acceptance with every voting bloc.

Past and current generations of politicians have left us with massive debt and few options. The political upheaval that will emanate from any future round of serious inflation will likely be profound, and perhaps tragic in the form of a vengeful and emotional public. Younger "baby bust" generations saddled with the costs of maintaining older americans in luxurious benefits, and paying heavy taxes with devalued dollars, will not feel such generational obligations have been sanctified by "clean" and responsible politicians. Changes will be made.

If, for example, the current generation of re-electable politicians is unable to solve our federal deficit problems, or even accede to the demands of a bipartisan commission on the debt, and we enter another financial crisis period similar to the depression, only at that point of desperation will new political parties begin to acquire legitimacy and become viable. However, as history amply illustrates, this is usually the wrong time to attempt reform. It is often only during the throes of a crisis when the opportunity arises for substantive change. Hitler, of course, emerged out of the ashes of the German depression at a time when the psyche of the people was ripe for radical change due to the ravages of war and economic suppression due to crushing reparations programs. Fascism feeds on discontent and political ineptitude.

Longer single terms will make legislative responsibility possible under the toughest of political conditions. And with longer terms our representatives can not only be more independent in office but they are apt to gain a greater sense of service and accomplishment from their term of government service.

In addition, the longer single terms of a one-term solution will open the arena to qualified candidates without previous political experience. The sad truth is that our system now excludes more able candidates than it includes. In fact, the very purpose of a single-term proposal is to open the candidate selection process to a wider group of individuals who do not feel contrained by the fact that they have never held elective office. America is blessed with a deep and largely untapped reservoir of talent in business, the professions, and the arts. We have no shortage of capable candidates for office. We only need change our representative system for this talent to emerge.

AMENDING THE CONSTITUTION —

> "The Congress, whenever two-thirds of both houses
> shall deem it necessary, shall propose amendments
> to the constitution, or, on application of
> legislatures of two-thirds of the several states, shall
> call a convention for proposing amendments,
> which, in either case, shall be valid to all intents
> and purposes, as part of this constitution, when
> ratified by the legislature of three-fourths of the
> several states, or by conventions in three fourths
> thereof, as the one or the other mode of ratification
> may be proposed by the congress."[40]

Article V, United States Constitution

From the 1st thru the 86th Congress (1789 to 1960) a total of 5,225 proposals to amend the constitution were brought before the House. The fact that we have passed only 23 Articles of Amendment since the founding of the republic is evidence enough of its hallowed status and limited use. Amending the constitution requires ratification by three quarters of the states - a feat not easily undertaken or achieved. It is difficult by design and intention - perhaps too difficult.

But that is not to say that we, the people, should not prevail upon this method of direct legislation to break open the legislative logjams created by politicians and powerful special-interest groups whose interests may run counter to the nation as a whole.

Some state legislatures today fear the idea of ratifying another Constitutional Convention because it means not only letting the people vote directly on matters of organization and principle but sifting thru hundreds of other less deserving and perhaps more divisive proposals. Yet these same legislators are sworn to uphold the constitution and accede to the wishes of their constituents. But "upholding" does not mean to preserve the constitution for all time in its present form and prevent utilization of the amendment process.

How do we get a hold on our government? In recent times it does not appear that voters have had the will to really use and experiment with the constitution. Rather, we appear to place it upon an altar and pray to it.

Is the constitution a living document or simply an icon?

What good is our constitution if the United States is destroyed economically by legislative irresponsibility? Out of necessity will the head of the Federal Reserve be forced to become de-facto president with legislative veto powers? And must we wait until faction, revolution, and state succession plans are well underway to consider constitutional remedies? Or should we have a periodic convention, say every twenty five years, to reconsider our past and our future? Considering the healthy effects of discontent, Thomas Jefferson once remarked: "God forbid we should ever be twenty years without such a rebellion."[41]

The fact that we have seen fit to modify and add to the constitution over twenty times in two hundred years is evidence enough of the necessity to be able to alter the document when times and conditions change. What the framers didn't foresee is the present day antagonism between career-oriented incumbents and the very people they represent - our interests run in opposite directions.

The practical impossibility of getting ratification from sufficient state legislatures to call a constitutional convention in our day and age is sufficient reason to consider making the process mandatory if the people are ever able to get another chance at amending the document they cherish. But will we be able to alter the constitution when, to call a constitutional convention, we have to go thru the very hard-core careerist legislators that we may want to bypass, or even eliminate? If career-oriented legislators in enough states sense that a one-term solution is likely to surface at a new constitutional convention will they prevent it from occurring? Could this be the catch-22 of our modern day republic?

Why is there so little discussion today about the potential for fundamental changes in our political system? Have years of saluting the flag and worshipping the constitution dulled our ability to examine the real world? Has mind-numbing recitation of the pledge of allegiance hypnotized us into thinking we have effective government? Can we not now act with the same audacity and intelligence as our forefathers to solve our own pressing problems? Have we been brainwashed beyond redemption into accepting a structure of representation that has outlived its usefulness?

In many ways, time has passed the constitution by. Our technology has transformed the document in ways unforeseen by its creators. Once again it is up to the people to re-vivify the document in ways that enhance the direct power of the people and ensure the responsiveness and responsibility of the Congress, Senate, and the Executive branch.

If any one issue today cries out for a constitutional amendment it is that of a balanced federal budget. The federal budget process and deficit spending are simply out of control. Decades of politicians have now, literally, passed the buck on fiscal responsibility to future generations whose only option is likely to be inflation and a painful domestic devaluation of the dollar. De-facto devaluation has already taken place in international markets as we continue to spend ourselves into an illusory "prosperity" with tax money belonging to another generation.

Indicative of our present dilemma is the fact that Social Security "trust" funds are now being diverted to lessen budget deficits. During the Reagan era, a new generation of politicians, while pledging "no new taxes," has supported a near doubling of the wage-earner's and employer's social security contributions. At the same time, these "trust funds" are then "borrowed" to lessen budget deficits and replaced with I.O.U.'s to be repaid by a new generation of taxpayers. Such budget chicanery is ultimately the financial rape of one generation by another.

It may be that amendments to our constitution are the only way to chasten our representatives and unlock the impasse in our legislatures. Constitutional amendments and national

47

initiatives are the only feasible approach for voters to directly change the rules of the political game and bypass recalcitrant legislative bodies and, where necessary, our judiciary. And short of a revolution in human nature, a one-term constitutional amendment for congressmen, senators, and the presidency would be a good beginning.

INITIATIVES - BYPASSING OUR LEGISLATURES

> "The initiative process, unique among our democratic rights, is founded on the belief that the citizens of this country are indeed as competent to enact legislation as we are to elect public officials to represent us."[42]
>
> Sen. James Abourezk

The history of direct democracy, of the people legislating directly, reaches far back into antiquity to the assemblies of Greek city-states and the plebiscita of Rome. The more recent tradition of referenda stems from the populist politics of Swiss Cantons as well as the lively Town Hall politics of our original thirteen Colonies. And by the end of the eighteenth century the developing ideology of democracy had legitimized the recall, initiative, and referendum as effective tools against errant public officials.

In the United States, with the exception of Delaware, all states have adopted some form of constitutional referendum, constitutional initiative, statutory referendum, or statutory initiative. Forty-five states require approval of constitutional amendments only by simple majorities. Thirty-nine states have some form of statutory referendum with twenty-four having the most liberal version requiring a ballot referendum when a certain percentage of voters submit a certified petition.

The greatest use of initiatives now occurs in the western states where the pioneering spirit of independence still runs strong. All fifteen states with pure legislative initiatives are located in the west. Oregon, California, Colorado, North Dakota, and Arizona generate by far the largest number of initiatives.

48

But it is becoming increasingly evident to voters in virtually every state that only the people, legislating directly, will effectively reform their government.

Statewide initiatives became necessary due to gridlocked legislatures and the unreliable "representation" of legislators willing to put their own interests ahead of their constituents. The truth is that the voters are often way ahead of their reelectable legislators who remain fearful of spearheading change and antagonizing any interest group. In fact, state referendums have been very instrumental in promoting civil rights, protecting the environment and consumer interests, as well as reforming the nature of civil service and elective office. California's Proposition 13 tax-revolt is the best example of voters taking legislative matters into their own hands after suffering the folly of arrogant career bureaucrats and bought-off legislatures.

Without the right of initiatives and referendums today, all voters would be virtual prisoners of special-interests and career politicians. However, on a national level, we are still prisoners of Congress, the Senate and the Supreme Court. As voters have done with their state constitutions, the time has now come to bypass the national legislative bodies by amending our federal constitution to permit nationwide initiatives.

We have the power. The First Amendment to the Constitution states: "Congress shall make no law abridging the rights of the people to petition the Government for a redress of grievances."[45] Petitioning is the people's form of legislating. And as Irving Wallace and David Wallechinsky point out: "The founding fathers would applaud a national initiative, particularly in view of radical changes produced by events of the last 200 years which make it more feasible - a once rural society gone urban, shifts of power, a technological revolution tht has brought with it sophisticated communications systems. Why shouldn't the voice of the people be heard when opinions can so easily be collected and evaluated by computer?"[46]

In 1977, after witnessing the success of state initiatives, senators James Abourezk and Mark Hatfield sponsored a bill to permit National Initiatives. Under the Abourezk-Hatfield plan, if a proposed national initiative received signatures of 3% of the voters in at least 10 states, it would qualify for the ballot in the next election. Unfortunately, their proposal died even though polls at the time showed 57% of americans favored the idea.[47] And most legislators dislike competition, especially from their own constituents. The battle for a nationwide referendum will not likely find many supporters in Congress.

Certainly any form of direct legislation is not without its problems. But recent experience with states utilizing statutory initiatives appears to refute objections that somehow this form of direct democracy will result in more inappropriate legislation than is already fed to voters by our special-interest controlled assemblies. In fact, most ill-conceived initiative proposals never make it to the ballot. Of those that do, given the facts and adequate media exposure, generally the good sense of the voting public will prevail.

It is also important to remember that any initiative can still be challenged and overturned by the courts. And depending upon the way a national initiative amendment is written, the vote could be subject to congress itself overturning the decision, given a high majority vote requirement to justify overriding the direct will of the people. Any system is subject to abuse, but the real question is whether or not there are adequate measures available to change the system.

Who will propose or write national initiatives? Certainly the worthiest of concerns can be damaged by poorly written and unbalanced ballot initiatives. But various factions affected by legislation could have their imput prior to the drafting of ballot issues, preferably by bi-partisan committees, to avoid lengthy court battles should the initiative be passed. And special-interest sponsored initiatives (a growing problem with many state referendums) would be unlikely to emerge without substantial review and imput from properly structured bipartisan review committees. The problems found in state initiatives, where there is inadequate public exposure as well as disclosure in the petition gathering period, would then be avoided.

A legitimate fear of utilizing state-wide and national initiatives is that big business and powerful special-interest groups will be able to control the process with money and confuse the voters with specious media campaigns. Given the fact that this is now being done with our legislator's election campaigns, there is certainly truth in this claim. The truth is that much legislation today is virtually dictated by special-interests and rammed thru legislatures.

But special-interest backing of initiatives is usually more transparent and discernable to the average voter than is the case with the campaign financing of candidates. This fact alone, along with the forceful and balanced participation of the media, aided by powerful disclosure laws, will keep the initiative process honest.

The real strength of initiatives is that they serve to empower voters and encourage participation in government by a larger segment of people who may be motivated by single issues, while at the same time generally unresponsive to the traditional insider single-slate type party politics.

In effect, initiatives are direct democracy in action. As Ralph Nader observed: "It's important that the ultimate check in a representative democracy is not revolution. The ultimate check is direct democracy."[48] To some, however, the initiative approach is more direct democracy than they feel is necessary or prudent. Columnist George F. Will stated: "The people are not supposed to govern, they are not supposed to decide issues. They are supposed to decide who will decide."[49]

Do voters really decide who decides? The voters, before the primaries, have little say in who emerges into our political campaigns. The truth is that financiers of campaigns dictate who runs. And what some candidates are willing to do to get on the ballot would, were it generally known by the voting public, surely eliminate them. Of course, once these "candidates" are in the race then we must pick from amongst a group of

51

whom few or none might ever have been nominated given more bipartisan and democratic nomination procedures.

Regardless, the issue of initiatives in a representative republic calls into question the ultimate wisdom of the people. We might answer this critical question by asking how "we, the people" would have decided important issues, via initiative, in the recent past? As David Wallichinsky and Irving Wallace point out in their study of referendums, if a national initiative law had taken effect in 1950, the following people's legislation would have been enacted thru 1980:

* "By 1952 party conventions would have been eliminated, and presidential candidates would be chosen instead by a nationwide primary.

* In 1953 the voting age would have been lowered to 18 (The politicians didn't get around to doing this until 1971.)

* By 1965 all electric and telephone wires would have been moved underground.

* The Electoral College would have been discarded by the mid-1960's, and presidential elections would be decided by direct popular vote.

* In 1969 it would have become illegal to heckle. In the same year, compulsory national service would have been instituted, giving young men the choice between military and nonmilitary service.

* U.S. troops would have been withdrawn completely from Vietnam by the end of 1970 (this would have saved 4,852 American lives, kept another 60,000 Americans from being wounded, and prevented over 400,000 Vietnamese, Cambodian, and Laotian casualties.)

* The Equal Rights Amendment would have passed in 1975.

* The draft would have been reinstituted in 1980, with women included.

* The government would be legally obligated to balance the federal budget.

* There would be public funding of congressional campaigns, and no private contributions would be allowed."[50]

Not a bad list of accomplishments had voters been allowed to legislate by initiative and directly affect their own future. In just one instance, literally trillions of dollars of wasteful spending would have been saved by the passage of a Balanced Budget Initiative over a decade ago. So the people as a whole, via their own iniatives, have demonstrated they are capable of legislating wisely when necessary - if only we had.

It is imperative that voters now pressure congressmen and senators into passing enabling legislation for a National Initiative. Otherwise the process of evasion and postponement, fostered by special-interest financed politicians, may go on indefinitely. While it may be easy for powerful lobbyists to influence 535 congressmen, or 100 senators, to influence millions of voters is another matter. The reality of the initiative process is that the vast majority of voters don't have a vested interest in seeking or remaining in office. Nor would most have a direct financial or political interest in most initiatives, save those of a direct taxation issue such as Proposition 13.

In theory, and in practice, the votes of the body politic will likely be purer than that of legislators with long lists of contributions from interested parties. This is plainly evident given the interests and obligations of candidates now spending a million dollars to campaign for a job that pays $45,000 per year! In California, for example, twelve state legislature contests in 1986 cost each candidate over one million dollars, and five cost over two million each. These alarming figures dwarf the annual salary of these state legislators. One wonders what is being bought, and what is being sold?

In the end it is the failure of legislators to enact any meaningful spending limits, or reform, that forces voters to act thru the initiative process. And the prime instrument of true trickle-up democracy is without doubt the direct initiative. But the fears of the framers regarding such "direct democracy" were overstated even in their day. Today, however, we are haunted by our principles of one-man, one-vote and making "liberty and justice for all" a reality.

And now technology forces the question of whether we even need full time, career-oriented, legislators? In the new era of electronic voting, perhaps all we need are legal scribes and a police force

Unfortunately, when we examine the apathy among voters today, we might come to a new appreciation of the republican, or representative, form of government. Certainly some issues are subtle and complicated, and a certain expertise is needed. But given proper debate, expertise will emerge for the body politic to ponder. When voters no longer feel excluded from the legislative process, and manipulated into voting for candidates with suspect campaign financing, we will surely see a rebirth of interest in exercising the vote. Common sense is more prevalent than politicians care to imagine.

Would any potential "abuse" of the initiative process be worse that what we have now? Restricted to major issues, and certain structural reforms, the use of initiatives are invaluable - if for no other reason than to demonstrate to our legislators that power ultimately resides with the people.

Why not single-term initiatives? This may be the only way effective political reform is possible, either on a state or national level. This particular reform must come from the people. The prospect of serious political reform coming from legislators themselves, given our method of campaign finance, is highly unlikely for all the aforementioned reasons. And the probability of incumbents voting for a single-term initiative is remote to say the least.

A National Initiative will give voters a way to legislate directly at periodic intervals, say presidential election years.

And if thru a single-term initiative the political career incentive is removed, and the lurid spectacle of grubbing for reelection funds eliminated, a new class of talented people might be drawn to public office and the prospect of better and more responsible government greatly increased.

THE ONE-TERM PLEDGE —

"In 1958 the two traditional political parties of the South American nation of Columbia concluded a unique bargain. Having regained their country from dictatorship only to confront economic despair, they agreed upon an unprecedented sixteen-year National Front Coalition. Every four years, for sixteen years, the presidency was to be alternated between the two parties. Each of the four Presidential cabinets and all appointments were to be divided equally between the two parties. And lower level officials were for the first time to be selected on the basis of merit. Neither party under normal circumstances would willingly surrender the Presidency after only one four-year term. But both parties adhered to this bargain for sixteen years. Domestic violence was contained. And economic development did go forward. The Columbian Coalition was a success. By each party refraining, for that limited period, from its insistence that the country go its way or no way at all, and by each party submitting to cooperation and compromise for a fixed number of years, the country was saved from disaster. As former President Alberto Lleras Camargo said, the coalition's purpose was to 'do everything that the two parties had said should be done, but that each had not allowed the other to do.'"[51]

Theodore C. Sorensen

Political gridlock and reelection fever are not exclusively american problems. In desperate times, as Ted Sorensen pointed out, nations may be forced to institute an informal single-term arrangement to eliminate political gridlock.

In Columbia's case, a one-term, and one-party, political arrangement took the form of a voluntary coalition. Under this arrangement, access to power for both factions was shared and effectively guaranteed. The major political parties could then cease to exist as simply warring factions and become partners in solving problems and peaceful transitions. In effect, Columbia recognized the need for a one-term solution.

Short of statutory and constitutional changes requiring massive and sustained grass-roots political efforts, another effective way to achieve the same result is to make a single-term process voluntary. As in the case of Columbia, a candidate, or party, simply gives the people their one-term pledge. If they should subsequently succumb to reelection fever their obvious lack of restraint and integrity would, in the eyes of the voters, disqualify them from further time in office.

This type of arrangement is particularly suitable where two political parties predominate. The importance of a single-term pledge can best be understood in the light of the vast machinery of government and bureaucracy that is currently brought to bear to guarantee the perpetuation of the party in power. The awesome ability of the party in office to manipulate perceived reality includes the ability to re-define, re-categorize, and "finesse" important economic statistics while indulging in self-serving budgetary chicanery. One party can "spend us into prosperity", or simply let entitlements soar out of control, and thus set the stage for the calamity of the next administration.

Unfortunately, the process of reelection necessitates, for reasons of political survival, the denial, postponement, and avoidance of real problems and their solutions. Political survival dictates that there is much to gain and little to lose by cheating the future. In contrast, single-terms would, in my opinion, encourage more immediate response to problems. Whether by statute or pledge, a single-term coalition approach to better government could solve our american political dilemma.

Sorensen's prescription for a "Coalition Administration" embodies the essence of a single-term approach to government. Coalition politics is essentially the politics of problem solving as opposed to party power and personal careerism. As Sorensen concluded: "A consensus-building president will be less dogmatic, less ego-centric and less rigid than some of his predecessors; but he will be no less the leader of the government and nation."[52] As the chief executive and leader of all the people, the petty party building activities of recent presidents is surely beneath the dignity of the office. As Sorensen states, there is a higher calling for the president:

> "The President in a Coalition Administration must be perceived by the Cabinet, the Congress and the nation as acting without partisan motives. He must relinquish the traditional role of party leader. He must abolish the traditional White House staff position overseeing party activities. He must renounce the traditional Presidential prerogative of selecting and replacing his party's National Chairman. He must avoid the party fundraising dinner circuit. He must refuse to make partisan campaign speeches, either in midterm or at term's end either for any member of his party who has not wholeheartedly supported the Coalition or against any member of the opposition party who has wholeheartedly supported the Coalition. He must, in his press conferences and speeches, avoid any partisan claims or attacks. Most important, he must prove his good-faith committment to bipartisan coalition by declaring from the start that he will not be a candidate for reelection."[53]

Sorensen's recommendations clearly suggest another experienced political participant has recognized, in effect, the need to eliminate the destructive process of reelection. All of this partisan activity that sullies the majesty of the office is simply the result of the reelection syndrome and party politics. In Sorensen's scenario, coalition and consensus building must ultimately replace party politics if we are to progress from the schoolyard antics so common in today's election contests.

The time has come to jettison the puerile "us versus them" mentality of traditional two-party politics. We must set more appropriate lengths on the terms of political office and, short of a constitutional ban on reelection, require our candidates not to look beyond a single term. Let them simply take the one-term pledge. If they refuse voters can quickly dispense with their candidacy.

And the coalition approach is not without precedent in the turbulent history of the United States. In 1864, Abraham Lincoln was faced with a country in the midst of a civil war. And to emphasize the bipartisan nature of the task of saving the union, Lincoln persuaded the Republicans to rename their party - a considerable feat. Thus, the National Union Convention emerged as a step toward coalition during our civil war.

Lincoln also took the drastic but adroit step of nominating Andrew Jackson, a leading democrat and head of the opposition party, to be his vice-president. Indeed, Lincoln was serious and desperate for unity and national reconciliation. Never before had a candidate voluntarily chosen a member of the opposite party for his running mate. But these were not normal times. Lincoln knew the time had come to stand above party politics. Andrew Jackson, sensing the importance of the arrangement, agreed to combine forces with his political enemy in order to save the union. Coalition is possible even in the worst of times.

If we examine the history of the Twelfth Amendment to the Constitution, ratified in 1804, we find that it was adopted to change the original practice whereby the victorious President candidate would normally chose, as his vice-presidential running mate, his main rival. But the unsuccessful pairing of John Adams with Thomas Jefferson led to the amendment and a change in the method for selection of a vice-president. Regardless, the consequences of that unfortunate pairing should not blind us to the framers original idea of coalition in blending winners and losers in a workable format. Exclusion of candidates losing by the narrowest of margins from any political participation is not only impolite but impolitic.

The problem with our winner-take-all elections is that we wind up with 51% dictators, a major stumbling block to coalition government. The major parties maintain a lock on access to power in these arrangements. In the aftermath, the 49% "losers" are symbolically and sytematically castrated. Is this majority fascism necessary or desirable? As Madison stated in Federalist 51: "it is of great importance in a republic, not only to guard against the oppression of its rulers, but to guard one part of society against the injustice of the other part."[54]

The total exclusion of "losers" from the political process, along with the ideas they represent, is what inevitably produces unprogressive see-saw politics. Progress is stymied by majority fascism and consensus is blocked. Compromise and coalition is seldom on the minds of successful candidates the day after an election. The ego concerns of "winners" poison and clog the legislative pathways. Even those winning by the most narrow of margins, even pluralities, claim they somehow have the "mandate" of the people. This is especially galling when we consider that the "winner" can be "one who gets 51 percent of the vote cast by 40 percent of the 60 percent of voters who registered."[55]

A more rational and democratic system of proportional representation, along the lines of parliamentary democracies, would allow minority parties power according to the percentage of overall votes. Greater fairness and diversity in representation will more clearly reflect the public will, increase political participation, and facilitate successful coalitions. Instead, what we have today is the obstructionist tactics of losers pitted against the aggressive behavior of the winners. The legislative stalemates produced by see-saw politics can last entire terms of office to the lasting regret of voters.

Coalition politics is the politics of the future. In the past it has been the only successful approach to politically hot issues such as fundamental changes in the Social Security system. Recent experience has shown that only bipartisan coalitions, that equally distribute or nullify partisan political damage, can "take the heat" and produce effective legislative solutions to our problems. In each such case our legislatures have recognized their utter uselessness and abdicated their responsibility to bipartisan citizen groups.

What good then are re-electable legislators who cannot, or will not, legislate when necessary?

Sorensen is right, coalition simply needs more political exercise than we have allowed. Without it we may be destined to national decline thru a process once described as the "deadlock of democracy." And there is precedent enough for Americans to indulge in necessary political experimentation in order to form a "more perfect union."

CITIZEN-POLITICIANS —

> "We should revive the concept of the citizen-politician for whom service in Congress is a temporary diversion from a career in private life, rather than a career in itself."[56]
>
> Rep. William Armstrong

* * *

> "There was a time when serving in congress was seen as a patriotic duty, akin to serving in the armed forces in time of war. Successful men and women would take time from the pursuit of their careers in private life to give their country the benefit of their wisdom and experience. The hours were sometimes long, and the pay was not good; but they were performing a public service. And, lawmakers intended to return to private life after a few years. Today we are now in the era of the professional politician, the career lawmaker; and too many of them view public service as a lifetime ride on the gravy train, with the taxpayer paying the fare. Turnover in Congress used to be farely frequent. In the first 40 years of the republic and

60

average of more than 40 per cent of the House members was replaced every two years. In the mid-1950's 15 to 20 per cent was typical. Today, once a member is elected, there's a good chance he's in for life. In 1976, 97.3 per cent of House incumbents who ran were reelected."[57]

Rep. David Treen

Former Representatives William Armstrong and David Treen are not the only ones to come to the conclusion that something is rotten in Congress. However, the only sure way to break the vice grip of incumbents upon our political system is by constitutional amendment, or national initiative, to limit and lengthen the term of office. By doing so we also decrease the number and cost of elections and increase participation in politics by non-career politicians.

We can differ on the prescription for the remedy, but upon the validity of the illness there is little dissent. Without a return to the ideal of participation in government as service, we are destined to continue with a system of advantages and attraction to incumbency that paralyze the office-holder with thoughts of losing such hefty perquisites.

We have allowed to flourish a system where the motives of self-interest work to to stifle the interests of the people. But the motives for serving, volunteering, or participating in a particular cause are fundamentally different from those in which we expect to profit while carving out an ego-media-profile and generous remuneration at public expense. I am not advocating a flacid and geriatric government of only retired businessmen, but a more dynamic body politic where a leave from one's business or profession is looked upon as something normally done at an opportune juncture in one's life. We must open the political arena to all - government is simply too important to be left to career politicians.

"Who are to be the objects of popular choice? Every citizen whose merit may recommend him to the esteem and confidence of his country. No

61

qualification of wealth, of birth, or religious faith, or of civil profession is permitted to fetter the judgment of disappoint the inclination of the people. If we consider the situation of the men on whom the free suffrages of their fellow-citizens may confer the representative trust, we shall find it involving every security which can be devised or desired for their fidelity to their constituents."[58]

James Madison

It was the fervent hope of the writers of our constitution that the union they created would be vivified by new generations of citizen-politicians from all walks of life. They took great pains to design a political system that would be free of the privileged political aristocracy such as surrounded the King of England. But like all political solutions, our constitution simply represents a compromise possible over two centuries ago. The devices to protect us from the evils of political careerism have proven inadequate.

"Every security that can be devised" might well include a single-term limitation to prevent political corruption. Madison would likely concur with any amendment that rearranged the number and length of terms of office to promote "fidelity" to national interests as well as to those of one's constituents. Any change securing a representative's freedom from special-interests, and wildly excessive campaign costs, would be desired. And certainly any change prompting a greater number of people to participate in politics would be welcomed.

Madison's viewpoint about the people's ultimate use of our constitution was a dynamic one - it is there to be used. When political conditions warrant action and change, we should not shrink from change and necessary constitutional amentments merely from the dead weight of tradition.

In supporting a dynamic view of the constitution, Madison inquired: "why is the experiment of an extended republic to be rejected merely because it may comprise what is new? Is it not the glory of the people of America that, whilst they have paid a decent regard to the opinions of former times and other nations, they have not suffered a blind veneration for antiquity, for custom, or for names, to overrule the suggestions of their own good sense, the knowledge of their own situation, and the lessons of their own experience?"[59] Experimenting with our Constitution, in the interests of better government, is our very heritage.

Today we sense that the "restraint" of frequent elections, envisioned by the framers as a way of securing fidelity to the people, has outlived its usefulness. In light of the changes brought by modern media and the broadening of the electorate, we might even say it has backfired! Now, the necessity of frequent congressional elections only serves to undermine the efforts and fidelity of the representative while providing the illusion of possible success to a challenger easily overwhelmed by incumbent advantages. Citizen-politicians have little chance against our incumbent professionals today.

Given that the framers may not have foreseen the deadening effects of a two-party system gone stagnant with age and bureaucracy, they may well have had an overly optimistic view of human nature as it relates to elected, and re-elected, officials. The accepted rationale was that elections would be a cleansing affair where the people could exert their power. But today we more fully understand how our voting power has been circumscribed and reduced to irrelevance by the two-party nominating system and media power of the incumbents.

In considering "devices" to protect the electorate from their representatives, Madison also pondered over another crucial point: "what is to restrain the House of Representatives from making legal discriminations in favor of themselves?"[60] He had no answer to this fundamental question because there is little that can be done. And this is why we see "reform" legislation that amounts to little more than incumbency protection measures and salary increase proposals that would make a pirate blush.

Madison's somewhat improbable reply to this dilemma was that the "genius of the whole system" will somehow protect

63

us. But this is true only if we actually use that same "genius" to correct abuses of political office. "The genius of the whole system" is the people at work designing devices to secure their representatives fidelity.

Today, we might regard Madison as hopelessly idealistic. But he was dead right about the heart of the matter - we need to protect ourselves from our own legislators! And if Hamilton were alive today he would also question the effects and wisdom of short terms and the power of incumbency that so effectively discourages political participation by a wider group of citizens. Nevertheless, it was a somewhat naive faith in the curative power of elections that caused the framers to ultimately discard the idea of a single term.

But we should not also consider it heresy to state there may have been those at the Constitutional Convention who had their own opportunistic visions of lifetime political employment. Thus, to accept the notion of single terms only minimized their own future opportunities. In this regard, we could well be blinded by our own mythology if we do not accept the reality of such motives stirring among the delegates.

So if our current experience with ineffective politicians compels us to act with the same boldness as the framers of our constitution, so be it. Let us use the instrument of our freedom and salvation and not ignore the very provisions established for future generations to adjust the document to their time. Let us adopt a single-term initiative and re-invigorate our political process with citizen-politicians.

TRUE REFORM - ELIMINATING REELECTION

"More important than anything said by either Democrats or Republicans in the tiresome argument over congressional campaign "reform" is that long-term incumbency itself - for Republicans as well as Democrats - is more menacing to Congress than the PACs, which shell out to keep favorites of both parties in office and in line. Far better than a 'reform' of congressional

64

campaign funding would be a constitutional limit on the years any member could serve in Congress."[61]

Leonard Larsen

More political analysts today are beginning to sense the basic underlying defect in our political system - our problems are related to political careerism and reelection itself.

As we will explore in the following chapter, reelection, and the unending demands for campaign funds have literally given birth to many PAC's, or Political Action Committies, including those formed by the candidates themselves. In contrast, initial spending by challengers is often far below that of incumbents who have the advantage of raising money throughout their term to finance their reelection. The system is badly out of balance.

But reform is problematical. Recent efforts at federal campaign expense reform witnessed the absurd spectacle of a senator being bodily carried into the chamber to vote on a campaign finance reform bill against his will. In this instance, senate Democratic leader Robert Byrd of West Virginia sent out the capital police with arrest warrants when he could not gather a quorum to continue debate on a campaign finance bill. Senator Byrd stated that senators are paid "to vote... not to run and hide."[62] The moral of this little episode is that true reform by incumbent legislators may well be impossible.

This is not the first time a great nation's legislators have sunk to such depths. The experience of the ancient Greek and Roman cultures revealed that republics often disintegrate into factions of warring interests and self-serving politicians. Lionel Casson described the situation in the late Roman empire:

> "The ordinary candidate depended on direct bribery of individual voters. Bribery, in fact, become so taken for granted that voters regarded it as a right, a sort of annually recurring welfare payment. There was even a word for the agents who took care of passing out the funds, Divisores

(dividers) of the swag. Eventually the buying of elections grew so blatant that something had to be done about it, and various laws were passed whose purpose, like certain campaign laws we have today, was to limit the ways candidates could spend their money. In 67 B.C, for instance, it was made illegal to provide free treats for the voters. The penalty was not only a fine but a deeper threat - anyone found guilty could lose forever the right to run for office."[63]

Obviously, campaign finance reform has been an issue for centuries. But solutions can be elusive given human nature and the inherent defects in elective political systems. However, the pragmatic Romans soon came to understand the true nature of unrestricted democratic politics. They were forced to go for the politician's jugular - they eliminated the right to reelection. Losing forever the right to run for office - now that's true reform!

CHAPTER II

— CORRUPTION AND REELECTION —

"THE POLITICIAN AS AN INVESTMENT" —

> "The concentration of economic power, opinion power, and political power creates a sort of closed loop. Politicians must raise money from corporations in order to pay the networks the enormous cost of television time. Corporate advertisers call the network tune. And the networks must curry favor with the successful politicians to assure their franchise. The open society seems to be closing - not by conspiracy, but by this mutual dependence."[1]
>
> Kingman Brewster, Jr.

Two decades ago former Yale University President, Kingston Brewster Jr., accurately depicted our modern day political dilemma. Voters, and their legitimate interests, currently stand outside this new "loop" of political power. A powerful new symbiotic relationship exists between big money, big media, and big political power in the United States. And because it now costs millions of dollars to run for national office, campaign contibutions have become, in effect, investments in "licenses to govern the government."[2]

The new reality is that our political process, and the demands of reelection, serve to undermine the courage of the legislator. Given the present method and climate of electing our representatives, can voters expect to come out ahead of special-interests and PAC money? Will legislation reflect the true interests of the people, or the artfully concealed interests of those who pay the tab for re-election and legislative power? Is it possible for a legislator to remain uncorrupted under our present system?

Personal and parochial interests can easily overwhelm the interests of the whole. We have already seen how the reality of the sum of such compromises effectively "neutralize" solutions to our problems and eventually aggravate the general condition of our cities, states, and nation. The very process of reelection, campaign finance corruption, and political self-interest disturbs the balance of any community. But effective solutions to our common problems that conflict with the self-interests of the incumbent, and their major contributors, are not apt to make much headway. Multiply this tendency by all office-holders who seek reelection and you have a formidable force of politicians aligned against the public interest. Under our present system we are asking for government where our representatives are drowning in conflict-of-interest. Why?

"PAC-MEN" - SLAVES TO SPECIAL INTERESTS? —

> "Dependency on PACs has grown so much that PACs, not constituents, are the focus of a congressman's attention." Today the power of PAC's threatens to undermine America's system of representative democracy."[3]

> Rep. James Shannon

The interests of the electorate, as a whole, have been lost in the PAC-money shuffle of modern american politics. It must be said there is nothing inherently evil about Political Action Committees in that they are merely organizations of like-minded people involved in raising money for political purposes - a perfectly valid aspect of democratic politics.

But the influence of PAC's upon our political system is overwhelming and can hardly be called benign. This is especially true given that many PAC's are corporate, or union, sponsored and heavily funded. With their overwhelming financial power to "buy" expensive media-fought elections, representatives now seek PAC money to insure their reelection - it's just that simple and tawdry. But one wonders how many of our elected officials today, as recipients of large amounts of PAC money, could teach a high-school civics class with a straight face and a clear conscience?

It was soon after the 1974 Watergate scandal that Congress amended the federal election laws to limit the role of wealthy contributors and end secret payoffs by corporations and unions. In the Nixon era, former Commerce Secretary Maurice Stans and other fund raisers went so far as to set a quota of 1 percent of a wealthy man's net worth, or 1 percent of a company's gross annual sales as "expected" contributions to the Nixon campaign. Finally, the sordid disclosures and later conviction of Herbert Kalmbach, Nixon's personal "Bag-man" who picked up the multi-million dollar "contributions" from wealthy corporate elite, led to the passage of our current "reform" laws.

The new law formalized the role of PACs - Political Action Committees. The idea was that they would provide a legal and well-regulated channel for individuals to get together and support candidates. But as is the case with many well-intended reforms, there were unintended consequences. Instead of solving the problem of campaign financing, PACs have become the problem. They have proliferated beyond any expectation, and inject far more money into political campaigns than ever before.

Former cabinet member Joseph Califano believes PAC-money is undermining representative democracy: "The members become more responsive to the special-interests that are interested in what their subcommittee is doing than they are to their own constituents, because their interests are financing them. And there's far more money coming to people from out of their states and out of their district than ever before."[4] In effect, the affairs of many communities and entire states may be controlled by interests outside those areas! In these instances, the voting public may be completely out of touch with political reality.

With legislators now in alliance with campaign-funding special-interests, often from outside their states or districts, we have a truly untenable and unrepresentative situation. Now imprisoned by powerful PAC's and parochial interests Congress has become lame and unable to deal with the major problems of the day. Conservative columnist, Patrick Buchanan, recently noted this "collapse" of our Congress:

> "Congress's great energies are directed toward self-preservation. 90 percent of incumbents are now routinely re-elected. Voting themselves free direct mail, huge staffs, local offices, generous travel, and seizing a whip hand over the vast PAC millions - this year (1988), PACs are contributing to House incumbents over challengers by 100-1, members of Congress have become part of the permanent government. With the perks of Cabinet officers, they have the job security of GS-5's. While the country may move conservative, the Congress, immune to national opinion, goes on borrowing and spending America's wealth, transferring it to countless beneficiaries to maintain itself permanently in power. The only thing Congress has to fear is being courageous and, hence, controversial."[5]

Patrick Buchanan

Another observer of the campaign scene, Herbert Alexander, insists that the impact of PAC's is not really understood: "The decline of the parties is, in part, a consequence of election reform gone awry."[6] A candidate with powerful PAC's doesn't need a political party. The parties remain simply as nominating vehicles for candidates whom the PACs have already endorsed! It is these "candidates" that can now demonstrate they can mount and pay for a winning campaign.

70

Thus "winners" have money but they also have committments to PAC's - financial ties which ultimately tend to pervert their loyalty and may seriously compromise their effectiveness as legislators.

In other words, party loyalty has been supplanted by PAC loyalty - candidates need PAC-money more than they need a party. Senate campaign spending alone has increased from 38 million in 1976 to 179 million in 1986, the vast majority of which is now contributed by PAC's. Representative Thomas Downey put it more succinctly: "You can't buy a Congressman for $5,000. But you can buy his vote. It's done on a regular basis." Downey's candor is reflected by another colleague, representative Barney Frank: "It's a lot easier to raise money from PACs than from other sources... you sit there, somebody hands you a check for $3,000. and you say 'thank you.' "[7]

In 1986, for example, over 200 members of congress received more than 50 percent of their election financing from PAC's and special interests. Campaign costs have now reached the point where, as many have said, "only millionaires and special-interest candidates can get elected."[8]

Proponents of PACs say that the process of Political Action Committees simply funnels the money thru legitimate channels and keeps it from going in the back door. Certainly there is truth to this assertion, as well as the fact that PAC's represent the opportunity for large numbers of small donors to have a greater impact by pooling their contributions. But in terms of influence over a large number of voters, big business itself forms a very large and powerful constituency. If you simply count the number of employees, shareholders, and their spouses, there are between 50 and 60 million voters now associated with the nation's 1300 largest corporations. This is just shy of the total number of people who voted in the 1984 presidential election! What's good for GM may well be what the country gets - whether we need it or not.

A well-known corporate journal, INC. Magazine, put it more bluntly in offering advice on 'some ways to measure your return' from PAC donations. They explained how to compute the 'equity-share' and 'cost-vote ratio' being 'bought' for each candidate: "Special interests don't contribute to congressional candidates for the fun of it... they do so to get things done." And any moral qualms are easily dismissed in this cost-benefit equation: "If politicians want to sell and the public wants to buy, there is not much you can do to stop the trade."[9] Now it seems PAC's simply "takeover" a candidate and make possible his or her reelection. Thus, the ethics of Wall street, so effective in carving up our business community, are also hard at work on our political process.

The problem with campaign finance "reform" generated by legislatures is that most reform bills are skewed to protect incumbents and stifle opponents - incumbents wind up with even bigger advantages. Republicans argue, however, that most of the people now in congress are Democrats and, consequently, it is Democrats who will benefit from "reform" and the excessive costs of campaigns will simply be shifted from PAC's to the taxpayer. But Democrats counter with the argument that present limits on campaign contributions are so riddled with loopholes they give new meaning to the term "limits."

With the exception of a few active reform groups like Common Cause, we have today a largely disinterested and disaffiliated electorate watching the single-issue specialists at work. Thru this process politicians divide and conquer the electorate and guarantee their reelection. Voters are cunningly manipulated into reelection of incumbents able to bring an entire political and media machine to their service in perpetuating their career. PACs and reelection are a deadly combination.

> "It is a law, sacred to me while in public character,
> to receive nothing which bears a pecuniary value.
> this is necessary to the confidence of my country,
> it is necessary as an example for its benefit, and
> necessary to the tranquility of my own mind."[10]
>
> Thomas Jefferson

How do we attract a new generation of office-holders with the standards and ethics of a Thomas Jefferson in today's sorry political environment? Without dramatic campaign finance reform, and a sheer limit on the number of terms and elections, the political game is not likely to change for the better.

Campaign money has become a drug. Political contributions are now "laundered" and sanitized like drug money. But if our politicians are hooked on reelection and PAC-financed campaigns, is there any possible rehabilitation? How do we detoxify our legislators? Can voters organize a mass withdrawal from these addictive symptoms in our system? Where is our "zero-tolerance" campaign on political corruption? It appears it is now up to voters to "just say no" to the process of reelection.

The ways and means of devious campaign finance are endless. Former lobbyist, Robert Winter-Berger, outlined current corporate tactics on political contributions: "many contributions are made by corporations - illegally. An officer of a corporation can personally contribute a flat sum to a candidate, but then his corporation can provide printing services, personnel, jet planes and automobiles. All these expenditures are then illegally deducted and charged off as business expenses. And contributions are made in cash. Illegal, yes, but done all the time. Dummy corporations are formed and, in most states, are not required to account for funds received or spent, so there is no way to trace the money. Contributions are disguised as loans that are never repaid, or are repaid only in part."[11]

Large donors who are able to hide their identities with these subterfuges provide the bulk of funds for our modern political campaigns. Candidates for Congress and the Senate soon find themselves beholden to a few wealthy contributors and that is the reason, as Winter-Berger stressed, "they have such power over the candidate when he wins."[12]

If the votes of our legislators always fell into line with their espoused philosophical positions it would be less easy to detect the influence of PAC money in politics. To illustrate the shifting ethical sands of certain conservative "laissez-faire" and anti-big government senators, Congress Watch conducted what they called a "Hypocrisy Poll." Results showed the members in question receiving more than 80 per cent of their "donations" from business related PACs.[13] But with regard to three votes covered in the study, they readily abandoned their free-market philosophy and voted for the specific government benefit sought by their major PAC backers - so much for philosophy.

How do our laws evolve? By whom, and for whom, are they made? Can we reasonably infer that some legislator's votes follow money, or does money follow votes? What is the cause and effect relationship? In fact, it may be both - money before and after the vote. Prussian Chancellor Otto Von Bismark was fond of saying that those who wish to retain their respect for laws, or sausages, should not watch either being made.

INCUMBENTS FOREVER —

> "In 1987 - a year in which no regular elections were scheduled (in California) - legislators raised more than 25 million... of that money, all but $400,000. was raised by incumbent legislators."[14]

Richard Paddock

The most honest and idealistic of new congressional and senatorial candidates and representatives soon learn that reelection demands the worst of compromises and scrutiny by special-interests. Representative Bruce Morrison put it bluntly: "All around you, you see your colleagues in Congress using the power of their incumbency to rake in money. And given those realities, what do you do? You have two choices: either play the game, or tie your hands by rejecting interest-group money."[15]

As long as we have multiple-term representatives, dependent on special-interests for the lion's share of their reelection campaign expenses, we are doomed. And regardless of party, the more meaningful fact is that more PAC money goes to incumbents than challengers in ratios as high as 100 to 1. Not surprisingly it is the issue of reelection and quid-pro-quo influence that this money speaks to. As Senator Joe Biden revealed: "Pac-money now underwrites the tyranny of the incumbent."[16]

The sheer power of incumbency, combined with PAC financing, can be glimpsed by the examining the results of recent elections. In 1986, in the state of California for example, out of 45 congressional races, 44 incumbents won. In 80 assembly races, 77 incumbents won. Journalist Eric Steele observed "145 races... and in 12 of them there was no incumbent, so the total that was possible for incumbents to win was 133 - they won 131! But even more startling is the margin by which they won. In only 14 races did the candidates finish within 10 points of each other."[17]

It is not outlandish to assert most incumbents would have to be arrested for rape prior to an election to give challengers any hope of victory today. Challengers, by the definitions of PAC-money politics, are both broke and invisible. But it is the electorate that is the real loser.

The reasons for such dominance by the incumbent, especially at the state level, are twofold: fund raising and gerrymandering. Added to the power of incumbents on-going fund raising abilities is the periodic redesigning of districts by incumbents to ensure reelection. Gerrymandering, or redistricting, is simply the incumbent's way of divying up the body politic such as to secure their reelection. Proof of this power of incumbency can be found in our state legislatures. For example, in California, the legislature has the power to summon up a small army of over 2300 employees whose salaries are paid by the taxpayers. The staff of state legislators work in capital and district offices and their livelihood depends upon the successful reelection of their boss. Here the overlap between state business, and personal campaign business, becomes increasingly blurred.

Having their own taxpayer-paid operatives in the field throughout their incumbency is a tremendous advantage for elected officials. Paul Jacobs explored the role of state legislator's staff during election campaigns and revealed the potential for abuse: "As long as the legislative staff members take unpaid leaves from their state jobs or do campaigning after hours, on weekends, or on vacation time, their politicking is legal. The problem is that it is difficult to prove whether legislative employees have, in fact, taken leave when they work on campaigns, particularly in the (state) Senate, which has instituted a policy of destroying leave and vacation records once an outside audit is completed each year."[18]

The results of this activity can be seen in the explosion of California legislative staff costs which have increased from 19 million in 1968 to over 181 million in 1987. Jacobs added that "some past and present legislative employees complain of what they see as increased pressure to participate in campaigns and to contribute to campaign coffers. They speak bitterly of a once-proud staff, now dominated by a corps of political operatives who devote their taxpayer-paid energies to keeping incumbents in office."[19]

Legislative analysts also are hired, in part, to develop "independent" and "nonpartisan" studies of issues and lessen the representative's reliance on lobbyist's bills and research. But they are under increasing pressure to participate in campaigns at all levels of public office today. The line between legislative analyst and lobbyist is also now blurred. One such analyst commented: "around the capitol, running for reelection is part of the business."[20]

No out-of-office challenger can mount a similar army of government paid help. Instead, the most opportunistic of challengers feel compelled to out-promise incumbents and hope to divert the same PAC money for their own campaign. In effect, the selling of the office begins well before the election. Worst of all, the average voter is little aware of the compromises and source of campaign funds of either the incumbent or any challenger until after the election. Meanwhile, the taxpayer-paid army for the incumbent marches silently forward fearing for their jobs and the outcome of the next election.

Corruption in our state legislatures has reached such proportions that the Federal Bureau of Investigation has taken to conducting "sting" operations on legislators - the same process developed for mafia criminals. In California, the FBI set up fictitious companies that gave legislators campaign contributions and speaking fees for speeches that were never given. And two lawmakers were reportedly videotaped accepting money before the sting was ended. The money was reportedly given for two obscure bills that would have benefited these bogus "companies" by allowing them to sell revenue bonds to finance their activities. Plainly, legislation was being bought and paid for. An attorney representing one of the defendants commented that the FBI decided to participate "because of rampant corruption in the Legislature and no one doing anything about it."[21]

ELECTION CRIMES & THE F.E.C. —

Supposedly overseeing our nation's campaign activity is the FEC, or Federal Election Commission. Created by the 1974 reform legislation, it consists of six commissioners, three Republicans and three Democrats, with four votes a necessity to act. The appointees are nominated by the administration, and approved by Congress. However, the commission, as presently constituted, is almost a sure bet to deadlock into paralysis and inaction. In fact, this seems to be the case today. The Federal Election Commission is destined to inaction due to the neatly conceived arrangements by Congress to produce a commission unable to act by the very nature of its constituency.

On the efficacy of the FEC, Common Cause observed: "Neither Congress, which approves FEC appointees, nor the administration, which gets to make them, is particularly eager to turn the commission into the campaign equivalent of the FBI. Thus many appointees are less than enthusiastic about the laws they are sworn to enforce. Anytime four commission members fail to vote in favor of making a decision, no decision is made at all."[22] With this setup the enforcement of election campaign laws becomes problematical and fertile ground for campaign finance lawyers.

To complicate matters, in the case of Buckley vs. Valeo, the Supreme Court undercut the efforts of the Federal Elections Commission! The court stated that since four of its members were legislative appointees it could not legally exercise legislative functions, or commence civil suits, without treading on the principle of separation of powers. In effect, a candidate who receives approval from the commission is virtually protected against any future prosecution!

It is apparent that enforcement of what "reform" exists is suspect. According to Common Cause; "When campaign finance lawyers aren't doing business directly with the FEC, they are unilaterally devising fresh interpretations of the FEC rules and regulations." As one FEC staffer explained, private attorneys "can give a stamp of approval (to a fundraising or spending scheme) without ever contacting the FEC." Naturally, in the rare instance when the FEC actually decides to look into a potential campaign violation, access to private counsel is essential. In the words of one FEC insider, "if you get into trouble, you gotta go to these people."[23]

The everyday reality of FEC "enforcement" actions is that staff recommendations regarding compliance are often overruled by the commissioners who, being fundraisers themselves, have no intrinsic desire to see the laws get too tough and interfere with their own activities. There is little inclination to abide by the spirit of the law - only the bare letter of the law.

So who's minding the store? When was the last time a Congressman was convicted of accepting a bribe, or a special-interest group of soliciting a politician to accept a bribe?

Sorting out the legalities of campaign activities has been left to a little known (because it's little used) agency. There is an obscure branch of the Justice Department entitled "Election Crimes Branch - Public Integrity Section" charged with overseeing our political system. They don't make the news much and the reason may be the very barriers Congress itself, and the courts, have placed in the path of prosecuting errant elected officials. One of the principle barriers is a little-known provision of the Constitution. Known as the "speech or debate" clause, Article I, section 6 states: "for any Speech or Debate in either House (members of Congress) shall not be questioned."[24] From this clause the courts have generally held that members of Congress cannot be questioned, or any evidence introduced concerning the propriety of his or her vote/debate in Congress or all "things generally done in a session" relative to legislative business. In other words, it is difficult to imply, much less prove, that any one vote was directly related to a contribution, as distinct from the representative's general philosophy.

This particular article derives from the British Bill of Rights and was rightly used to protect members of Parliament from the King when they voted in ways the Crown disliked. Originally, the idea was to protect the legislator from pressure on high, but not, perhaps, from the very people they purport to represent! Nevertheless, the effect is to make it impossible to convict or censure a member of Congress on a charge of bribery if evidence of trading a vote, in exchange for money or favors, cannot even be introduced. It is possible, however, for congressmen to waive their immunity in these cases but none are likely to do so.

Thus legislators on the take can easily hide behind the constitution, as currently interpreted by the courts. And, in addition, Congress shortened the statute of limitations to three years for campaign violations. In this environment, enforcement of our present laws is unlikely to lead anywhere or affect the outcome of any election.

Another design defect in campaign finance disclosure laws is the sheer volume of information required. It is virtually impossible for the media or public interest groups to sort thru the numerous federal and state disclosure reports *before* the election - when the information is vital! There are literally thousands of individuals and "committees" reporting campaign contributions. But there is simply too little time to analyze the information due to the fact that such a large percentage of donations are made in the days and weeks immediately predeeding an election.

Thus the media, or activist groups, are unable to get the facts out to the people before an election. And, after the fact, this information does the voters little good and arouses little interest. Scandals blow over until the next election. So the promise of disclosure as an effective reform tool is limited in its real impact.

"SOFT MONEY" & HARD POLITICS —

Years of exploring for loopholes and torturing the intent of campaign finance laws have resulted in a contribution concept called "soft money." The term refers to donations that cannot be used to elect federal candidates because they come from unions, corporations, or other sources prohibited in a federal election. But such "soft" donations can be used for "indirect" activities on behalf of a candidate. In 1978, the FEC reversed itself and ruled in favor of allowing state party committees to "use soft money for get-out-the-vote registration activities, even though it would effect the election of federal candidates."[25] And, as a consequence, so-called "soft money" is now being raised and spent in virtually unlimited "indirect" ways, and amounts, toward the election of federal candidates - so much for reform.

Common Cause noted that current law states: "individuals may give no more than $20,000 to a national party and no more than $25,000 all told to PACs, parties and candidates during a given calendar year."[26] But the Democratic National Committee accepted a $1 million contribution from the widow of Roy Kroc, the founder of McDonald's. How can this be legal? Why was it not returned?

The reason is that large donations are simply divided up into appropriate legal amounts and "stashed" in nonfederal "soft money" accounts. Where there's money, and politicians eager for reelection, there's a way. With these type of "legal" devices there are really no effective limits on campaign contributions. The Ronald Reagan years of campaign finance are looking more and more like the Warren Harding years in terms of campaign spending ethics.

STRUCTURE OR PERSONALITIES? —

> "America is not a plutocracy - at least not yet. But there were from day one, plutocratic tendencies, persons and groups who commanded wealth - or other forms of economic power - and who sought to use it to corrupt the democratic government. If you believe that in contemporary America it is the people, each person having an equal say, as in 'one person, one vote' you probably also believe in the tooth fairy. Plutocrats in a democracy work by corrupting public life. To corrupt is to change a sound condition to an unsound one. The unsound condition I deal with is the use of public office for private advantage. The main problem is one of structure, and not personalities. The problem lies in the American political system, because certain key elements of it - and especially those that legalize PACs - foster corruption on the part of lawmakers."[27]

Amitai Etzioni

Structure, and not personalities, is increasingly being recognized as the source of our current political problems. But merely changing the people in office, who are still subject to the same corrupt political environment, is unlikely to produce effective reform. In his book, Capital Corruption, Amitai Etzioni expressed his amazement at why Americans continue to focus on the personality cult of the individual rather than on reform of our "corrupt setup" when, in fact, it is the system that ultimately changes people.

Most astonishing to Etzioni is that the "most prevalent forms of corruption in contemporary America are legal."[28] It is this legal corruption in the form of money, gifts, payoffs, deals, honorariums, fees, junkets, and legal fees that may be within the current legal boundaries of our system, and mandated by our present campaign system, but yet are so astonishing. The ethical boundaries have been obliterated: "sizable campaign contributions (and fees) are basically unethical and largely undemocratic, because they make members of Congress focus on the sources of the funds rather than on the electorate, and all too often lead them to violate their sworn duty."[29]

According to former Representative Bob Eckhardt: "this process has all of the advantages of bribery and none of its risks."[30] And Representative John Breaux quipped: "I can't be bought... but I can be rented."[31] These legislative marriages of convenience prompted industrialist Justin Dart to comment: "with a little money, they hear you better"[32] So much for ethics.

Obviously, reform must not discourage voter participation in political campaigns, whether by contribution or donation of service. And unless we repeal the First Amendment, people and organizations with interests in legislation will be active. But the purpose of PACs is to influence specific areas of legislation pertaining to their sphere of interest. There is little question a quid-pro-quo is understood to be the reason for a contribution. To believe otherwise is to ignore the obvious. But contributions could easily be made direct to party organizations if the general philosophical stance of the candidate were the only concern.

PACs intend "rifle-shot" donations to specific legislators, regardless of party, to those most likely to effect the course of favored legislation. Former congressman, William Brodhead, once described the process as follows: "The legalities are observed. You're talking about very subtle people on both sides. But when they couple an invitation to meet their PAC director with a pitch to vote for such and such a bill, well, then its pretty clear... When we're all through talking about the legislation, they'll say, 'could you give me the address of your campaign committee?' These people who are contributing to these campaigns are not stupid - they're buying something.

It used to be a group would just agree with your philosophical outlook and would be willing to make the campaign contribution on that basis. Now votes are given in exchange for campaign contributions. That's what's happening around here."[33]

Unfortunately, that is the reality today. The problem for the body politic is getting Congressmen to seriously consider effective structural changes in representation. It is simply much easier to "go with the flow" and get the easy reelection money from PACs rather than raise thousands of small donations from luke-warm constituents. And there is even less chance these same representatives would likely consider a one-term solution to end their careers.

Further complicating matters is the fact that PACs are now affiliated with candidates, and not necessarily special-interest groups. It is these bogus "PACs" that spend millions of dollars for a candidate while he or she is busy not running! In this way candidates feel they can subvert the system by pretending they are not in the race while their own staffs are out setting up the campaign with funds "donated" to their own PAC's. This ruse is utilized because once the candidate declares his candidacy, all expenditures would be campaign-related and subject to disclosure limits of $5,000. And prior to the declaration of candidacy there is simply no limit on campaign contributions - loopholes abound.

"The campaign is never over"[34]

Robert Squier, Media Consultant

A little appreciated fact of our incumbent legislator's dereliction of duty is how much time they spend away from the affairs of their own constituents to campaign for re-election. One source reported Missouri Senator Dick Gephardt, in preparing for the 1988 presidential campaign, spent 144 "campaign days" in Iowa alone prior to the presidential primary. And that is only one of many primaries! "But technically Gephardt wasn't even running for president - not yet anyway. Then who was paying for Gephardt's trip to Iowa? Certainly not the Gephardt For President Committee, which did not at that time exist. Instead, it was paid for by the Effective Government Committee, which for all intents and purposes is Gephardt's personal Political Action Committee."[35]

The cynical ways that campaign laws are avoided appear to be legion. "Party Building" is a term used to describe the pre-campaign activities financed by the candidate's own personal PAC's to build the political base before the actual candidacy is declared. But this activity is a luxury reserved for incumbents or very well-heeled challengers. With names like "Campaign for America," Committee for America," "Fund for America's Future," "Campaign for Prosperity" these non-candidates finance their early campaign activities with money that is not even counted under the election laws ostensibly "enforced" by the FEC. This unreportable "indirect" campaign spending is a sham and a seedbed of political corruption. Early campaign work undertaken in the primary states is funded thru organizations that should be required to report their activities to the FEC. But as long as they call it "party-building" while they continue to pay for candidate's and campaign managers and their staff's travel expenses, direct mail costs, office rents, etc., they are within the law.

According to current FEC interpretations of campaign finance rules, these phony PACs are permitted what are termed "nonfederal accounts." And the only way to discover that these secretive accounts exist is to methodically search for reporting discrepancies between disclosure forms filed with the Federal Election Commission and those filed with state election offices. The FEC, it would appear, has no interest in doing this job, and they do even not keep records of "Nonfederal" accounts. Thus, effectively, there are no limits on campaign spending, and conversely, no limits on campaign taking.

We should also understand that much of today's political campaign funding is actually solicited, however coyly, and not necessarily donated. Wealthy individuals, corporations, and other special-interest groups are racked by the candidates and their advance men for funds. To blame special-interests and

PAC's alone for political corruption is to see only half the problem. The reelection-drugged candidates are clearly the other half.

As Watergate's "Deep Throat" suggested we should always "follow the money." And where does the money come from in most political campaigns? Today, with nonfederal, and thus non-reportable accounts, the candidate's own PAC can take money from anybody without any limits whatsoever. Any corporation, union, or other group can send as much money as they like to pay for these "non-campaign" related expenses. And that is not all.

Common Cause observed that "even money contributed to the PAC's 'federal' account has huge advantages. A crucial provision of public financing for presidential elections is that any individuals can contribute a maximum of $1,000 per candidate during the primary campaign. With PACs, that maximum is $5,000 per year, or potentially, $20,000 every four years. This can add up to a lot - especially if an individual's spouse and family members give the maximum as well."[36]

TAX-EXEMPT CORRUPTION —

Another major abuse in campaign financing occurs when tax-exempt foundations are used to raise money. In these instances, tax-deductible contributions are used for election campaign purposes in direct violation of the letter and spirit of the law governing charitable organizations.

While the tax code exempts certain educational, charitable, and welfare groups from paying income tax, it also forbids these same groups from political activities. However, this has not stopped presidential aspirants from setting up their own bogus tax-exempt organizations to provide a home for non-reportable, and tax-deductible campaign funds. Of course, the organization's stated objectives are purely charitable or educational. But they provide an irresistible opportunity to build a staff whose work often interrelates nicely with the candidate's own campaign.

In 1988, five presidential hopefuls, Pat Robertson, Gary Hart, Bruce Babbitt, Jack Kemp and Robert Dole set up tax-exempt foundations. The idea that all of these "foundations" were purely altruistic organizations stretches the credulity of the voting public beyond belief. A tax-exempt organization gives the candidate the ability to create a tax deduction for a political contribution; accept money from any corporate, labor, or even foreign treasury, and grant donor anonymity as the sources do not have to be publicly disclosed. The lure and advantages of tax-deductible contributions are just too tempting, and the abuse of this situation will surely continue until effectively stopped.

The exploitation of PACs and foundations has created a largely unregulated, and unreported, campaign spending free-for-all. With campaigns now spanning the entire term of elected officials, and presidential campaigning starting earlier every term, the abuses have become on-going.

Enforcement of even our loopholed campaign laws is almost nonexistent today. According to the FEC, whenever it finds that there is "probable cause" a candidate has broken the law, they are required to enter into a "conciliation" process with the alleged campaign violator. For example, to insure that the campaign finance process goes on unimpeded by voter complaints, Congress, in 1974, passed a confidentiality clause that would apply to such a hearing. But none of the information from the conciliation process can be made public by the commission! In one case, where the commission had probable cause to believe Ronald Reagan's PAC and campaign committee had violated the law, the conciliation process went on for five years and the fine, in the end, totalled $5,000.[37] How conciliatory can we get?

Only the voters, in toto, can avoid a conflict-of-interest in the reform of campaign financing. Otherwise, legislatures make their own rules and, as is often the case, simply fail to enforce the rules on its members. And reform legislation from within, from the unreformed, tends to be bogus. The inmates, as congressional behavior has demonstrated, cannot be counted on to control the process so crucial to their own political survival.

CAMPAIGN FINANCE REFORM —

The modern history of serious campaign finance reform began in 1907 with a law prohibiting national banks and congressionally chartered corporations from contributing to federal election campaigns. In 1910, Congress required all political committees operating in two or more states to disclose any transactions in excess of $100. Later, expenditure ceilings were extended to cover primary, convention, and prenomination efforts. In 1918, Congress finally made it illegal to influence voting with an offer of money.[38] In other words, it took nearly 150 years for Congress to outlaw political bribery!

In 1925, the Federal Corrupt Practices Act was passed to incorporate previous campaign finance reform legislation. In 1939 the Hatch Act prohibited political activities by federal employees. But political corruption continued to flourish, and public pressure forced Congress to impose expenditure ceilings on political committees and individual contribution limits. They were unwilling, however, to stop the proliferation of bogus committees organized for the sole purpose of evading expenditure limits - thus corruption continued.

Continuing scandal in presidential politics and public pressure eventually forced Congress, in 1966, to pass a $1 tax-checkoff presidential campaign financing plan. However, it was repealed in 1967. Four years later the Federal Elections Campaign Act revived the plan and required disclosure of all political contributions in excess of $100.[39]

In 1972, incredibly blatant influence peddling during the Nixon campaign highlighted the need for further reform. In one case, the Dairy industry, seeking to raise the government-paid price support programs, promised two millon dollars to the Nixon camp. But such a sum from a corporation or union was clearly illegal. However, the dairy industry offered to donate the money in $2500 amounts to virtually hundreds of political committees in various states to get around the law. Later, Nixon proposed higher price supports - thus the appearance of impropriety was complete.

Consequently, the 1974 "Watergate" reform act imposed new contribution, expenditure, and disclosure regulations as well as creating the Federal Election Commission to police campaign activity. The new law also took the important step of providing public financing for the presidential nomination and election process.

Less than a year later, however, the Supreme Court, in Buckley vs. Valeo, invalidated certain provisions of the new law. A majority of the Supreme Court somehow found reason to support the distinction between contributions, which are regulated, and expenditures on behalf of a candidate, which are not. The rational was that expenditures on behalf of a candidate are not as "direct" as contributions and are thus more a form of free speech and political expression protected by the First Amendment. In this decision the concept of "soft money" was born.

The American Civil Liberties Union delineated the full consequences of this decision by the Supreme Court: "In Buckley, the Supreme Court invalidated individual expenditure limitations as a "direct" interference with free speech. Thus, under current law, there are no limits on the amount which an individual may personally expend advocating the election of a specified candidate. After Buckley, a corporate or labor voluntary fund may expend unlimited amounts on behalf of a candidate so long as the funds are not controlled by the candidate. Thus, under current law, such corporate or labor committees wield enormous power. In Buckley, the Supreme Court invalidated all ceilings on the use of personal funds by a candidate. Thus a wealthy candidate may spend an unlimited amount on his or her candidacy. In Buckley, the court invalidated all expenditure ceilings on behalf of candidates. Thus, a candidate may now spend as much as he or she can raise. Since the law provides no public funding for Congressional or Senatorial elections, the court's decision now removes all restraints on expenditures in House and Senate elections."[41]

In practice, this dubious distinction means that a voter may be limited to a $1,000 contribution but may also spend an unlimited amount of money on a candidate's behalf as long as the expenditure in not under the candidate's direction and control. Today, it is apparent we have the appearance of campaign finance reform and not the substance. The average voter, the poor, the independent, and the unaffiliated are simply overpowered by the major parties and large labor and corporate organizations in our political arena today.

The effects of "reform" upon new parties and minorities has been devastating. Under current law, parties are divided into three groups: those with 25% of the popular vote in the last presidential election are deemed "major" parties; those with between 5% and 25% are deemed "minor" parties; and those with less than 5 percent are deemed "new" parties. But "new" parties receive nothing until *after* the election, and only if they receive 5% or more of the vote! The catch is that new parties cannot get matching fund money until they get the votes. In practice, however, they can't get the votes until they get the money!

Under this arrangement it is nearly impossible for anyone other than a Democrat or Republican incumbent to win office. No matter that the Supreme Court, in the 1968 case of Williams v. Rhodes, invalidated Ohio laws that made it virtually impossible for candidates other than Republicans or Democrats to get on the ballot. However, their choice of a 5% level of demonstration of eligibility, from votes garnered in a previous election, as an acceptable "threshold" or demonstration of public support, does not open the political process to new parties formed prior to an election, or popular "new" candidates sans party affiliation.[42] In other words, by this criteria, voters are stuck with the major party candidates and the status quo.

The effect of this 5% provision makes it almost impossible for alienated voters to escape the tyranny of the major parties. The reality is that an independent candidate for president cannot qualify for campaign subsidies despite the fact that they may have a pre-election majority in the polls! Thus the tyranny of incumbents and major parties, under current reform, is complete. The public's declining interest in politics and failure to vote is the result. Unless american politics are revitalized with significant reforms, we might soon see future elections where "winning" candidates receive a plurality consisting of a dismal twenty percent of the eligible voters or less.

PUBLIC FINANCING OF CAMPAIGNS?

"Campaign financing is a curse. It's the most disgusting, demeaning, disenchanting, debilitating experience of a politician's life."[43]

Hubert Humphrey

* * *

"The heart of the problem is the professional politician's insatiable need for campaign funds."[44]

Robert Winter-Berger

* * *

"Campaigns have become so expensive that, to wage a winning campaign, the average United States Senator must raise nearly $10,000. every week during his or her entire six-year term. Under the current system even the most idealistic senator has no alternative for achieving that task other than to rely on special-interest groups."[45]

Phillip Stern

Legislators, holders of the public trust, are now swimming in a sea of campaign finance corruption without adequate public support or censor. Can voters allow special-interest financing to pay for the bulk of expenses in our political process? Can we not eliminate most, or all, private financing of campaigns without violating our First Amendment rights? With prevailing Supreme Court dictum equating all political contributions with "free speech" we may never control political spending. We are lost in a sea of campaign finance technicalities.

We will not purify politics and get honest and effective goverment with our system of rampant reelection and campaign finance corruption. Some form of public financing, with limits on the length of campaigns and the amount of media expenses allowed, are needed to control the costs of running for office. With single terms, we can eliminate the advantages of political incumbency and continual fundraising. With public financing, compresssed campaigns, and more control of media access for public affairs, we can bring some semblance of order to what is now corrupt chaos. But any public campaign finance plan that does not somehow increase media access while, at the same time, limiting media expenses and the sheer length of campaigns, may be self-defeating.

Consider what we have today. The cancer of campaign financing works two ways. The normal method ivolves PACs giving money to candidates with an eye toward specific legislative benefits. The second, and less understood, method involves elected officials extorting money from these same PACs as well as other interested individuals and groups. One political fund raiser described the less than subtle extortion process of fund raising as follows: "You take a look at the campaign finance reports, and you say to XYZ Co: 'You gave the democrats $25,000. We (Republicans) normally vote for you, and you gave us only $10,000. This is inequitable. You've got to contribute more to us.' They need access, and they've got to respond in one way or another. So they very carefully sit down with their political action committee budget, and they very carefully allocate the money."[46]

This extortive process of campaign funding can take many forms. Any individual or group who has business pending before an agency, committee, or legislative body who is not already seeking ways to influence the outcome is often directly, or indirectly, solicited for "campaign" funds. What we have

91

today is a new brand of political extortion - mafia politics in the name of campaign finance.

The recent case of the former Mayor of Syracuse, New York, is case in point. A sixteen year incumbent, he admitted in a plea agreement to charges of racketeering, conspiracy to obstruct a government investigation (his own) and tax evasion. A 40-count indictment accused the mayor of 65 acts of extortion. The only explanation offered for his misdeeds was that his effort to build a political campaign war chest was "allowed to grow into a cancer."[47]

Distinctions between extortion, bribery, and campaign fund raising often disappear for incumbents blinded by ambition and self-serving dementia. They fail to see the distinction. This pandemic failure of politicians to refuse PAC donations when voting on measures affecting the particular PAC's interests is a clear violation of conflict-of-interest ethics. Unfortunately, not many politicians see it that way.

Powerful politicians can literally turn on the special-interest money tap with timely statements regarding legislation under consideration. As Hedrick Smith pointed out in *The Power Game,* "nothing galvanizes special interests like a major tax bill."[48] It is no wonder that Senator Bob Packwood, Chairman of the powerful senate Finance Committee, is known as "Mr. Special Interest" and the man who led the senate with more than $5 million in "donations" in 1985.

The power of incumbency places the extortive power in the hands of all politicians. But without reelection there is no need or reason! And in addition to money being placed into the hands of key politicians, PAC "donations" are sucked up by incumbents - a money vacuum cleaner works both ways. Given that there are no legal limits on the amount of money a PAC can give, combined with the fact that Senators and Congressmen can legally take the money with them when they leave office, we guarantee reelection corruption will continue.

Incumbents, worried about their political future, have also developed a "money scare-off" tactic spurring them to continually raise as much money for reelection as possible in the hopes that their campaign reserves will scare off any challengers. The "war chest" technique works - money talks.

Reelection is akin to a drug. We are witnessing today the addictive power of public office and all its trappings. And the substance abused is money. Our system currently supports and encourages these abuses. The motif of the modern professional politician is run, run, run, for office, and collect, collect, collect money until you do not pass go. The return to private life, and falling off the political gravy train, is seen by some as going "cold turkey."

Aside from a one-term solution, what is now necessary are new public campaign finance laws that set campaign time limits, expenditure and contribution limits, fair media coverage and access rules, and cover congressional and senatorial races as well as the presidency. Until we include the congressmen and senators in a workable form of campaign financing we will only continue to have special-interest government at the federal level.

All incumbents and challengers must be put on a level playing field, in terms of money and media available, spending limits, and debate requirements, or we will not have an open political arena. It is in the voters interests to prohibit federal candidates from receiving PAC money, especially from out-of-district political forces. Even though the Supreme Court has held that money is speech, the overriding public interest dictates that such limitations should be considered. We cannot allow PAC's to "assemble" votes as well as candidates and thus overwhelm legitimate local and national interests.

In most recent political surveys, a majority of the voters have approved of the idea of public financing of campaigns. Due to this sentiment the Presidential Election Campaign Fund Act became law. But the original tax return "check-off" plan was nearly scuttled by the Nixon republicans who perceived it as a direct threat to their traditional campaign funding advantage. The level of participation in the 1973 tax return check-off plan produced only 4 million in revenue for the Presidential election campaign. Although the 1975 participation rate jumped to fifteen percent of returns and produced 17.5 million, a 15% check-off rate was construed by many as a rejection of the concept by taxpayers.[49] But as voter's awareness of the vital significance of public financing increases, participation will likely increase and produce sufficient revenue.

In the 1988 California primaries, Common Cause spearheaded a successful drive to put a comprehensive Campaign Finance Reform Initiative on the ballot. The successful initiative imposed stiffer campaign contribution and expenditure limits as well as providing limited matching funds for candidates running for state Senate and Assembly. According to their estimates, the cost to each taxpayer for a system of matching funds would be about 17 cents a year - a small price for political reform.[50]

Even with total public financing of campaigns the problem of allocation of funding remains. How do we support new parties and maverick candidates who may appear outside of traditional parties? Should taxpayers check-off funds for a particular party years *before* they know who their candidate will be? Should new parties and independent candidates have to wait until after the votes are counted before receiving public grants while the major parties get theirs during the campaign! Flexibility and fairness are currently non-existent, and incumbents are unduly rewarded.

We also have a problem with "matching grants" where private money donations are matched with public funds. The current grant limit of $250 means that a rich donor triggers a full $250 of public funding for his dollar, while the voter donating $1 only triggers the same meager response. This is not exactly one-man/ one-vote equality. The widening income gap between the rich and the poor today reflects this very disparity.

Unfortunately, the threshold provisions to qualify for public matching grants require a candidate to raise a minimum of $100,000 with at least $5,000 coming from a minimum of twenty states. This twenty state provision was intended to discourage frivolous "favorite son" candidacies.[51] But consider, for example, the impact upon a popular governor or independent candidate, sans party, who did not run in a previous election and who may well be a qualified presidential candidate. It is virtually impossible for the public to "draft" a qualified candidate in opposition to the major parties and qualify them for federal matching grants. Despite their wishes, the public simply cannot match the current stranglehold of the "major" parties on our electoral system.

In effect, these fundraising hurdles discourage and prevent the sudden emergence, or spontaneous nomination by the voting public, of candidates other than those nominated by the major parties. The voting public continues to feel they are left with major party choices reflecting the "evil of two lessers." This twenty state requirement is especially unfair and nonsensical in view of the fact it is possible to win the Electoral College for president with only eleven states!

It is plain that our laws regarding public financing of political campaigns were hastily written and possibly purposely skewed to protect the major parties. Also, many provisions of these laws have yet to be challenged in court. Regardless of the eventual format of future laws, it is imperative that public financing be extended to congressional and senate races. It makes no sense to elect a president with "clean" public money while our representatives, with the power of the purse, continue to dwell in the netherland of PAC patronage.

However, if public financing remains available only for general elections, and not for primaries, we will have simply shifted the evils of private financing from the former to the latter. Financing is more crucial in the beginning than at the end of a campaign. This is especially true for independent and non-affiliated candidates. The nomination arena is where voters must have real influence and choice and all reasonable candidates given equal visibility. Otherwise the political process will continue with special-interest money controlling the voter's choice of candidates. Independent candidates as well as new political parties should receive their financing support in relation to the public's current support, or present poll standings, and not be limited to some prior election record which may not even exist.

Unless public support flows to candidates directly, and bypasses party control, we will never unleash our true potential to attract the best to public service. To date, obsession with party financing has only served to eliminate new parties and discourage individuals of merit. New reform must help equalize opportunities for all citizens to be heard and participate in the political process, while providing adequate financing, and media access, to assure all serious candidates a hearing before the voting public.

Can we afford broader public financing of our political campaigns? The truth is that we have no way of calculating the real costs to the voters of special-interest campaign financing. Although the extent of corruption fostered under the present system is incalculable, it is nevertheless substantial. Consider the cost of farm subsidies alone, and other pork-barrel favors, which dwarf any estimates of public finance of our campaigns. We have no choice but to pare and pay the costs of campaigns in order to regain control of government.

As Phillip Stern pointed out: "the cost of companion public finance bills introduced in 1985 was 87 million a year for the House and 49 million for the Senate. Both figures are much less than the Pentagon spends every year just on military bands! One expert has estimated that congressional public financing will cost around 500 million every two years, or 250 million a year. Even if the cost turns out to be twice that high - 500 million dollar a year - that will be just equal the added cost to the federal government of the higher dairy subsidy passed by the House after three dairy PACs showered congressmen and senators with over $1 million in campaign contributions."[52]

The lesson is clear. If we don't pay the direct costs of public financing of campaigns we will pay for it many times over indirectly in the form of subsidies and largesse to special-interests. The truth of the matter is that our priorities are simply absurd - there is no question that we can afford real reform.

CHAPTER III

— THE HUMAN NATURE OF POLITICS —

"AMBITION AND AVARICE" —

> "Sir, there are two passions, which have a powerful
> influence on the affairs of men. They are ambition
> and avarice, the love of power, and the love of
> money. Separately each of these has great force
> in prompting men to action; but when united in
> view of the same object, they have in many minds
> the most violent effects. Place before the eyes of
> such men a post of honor that shall at the same
> time be a place of profit, and they will move heaven
> and earth to obtain it."[1]
>
> Benjamin Franklin

Presaging the questions of many a modern day voter
about the nature of today's political aspirants, it was Ben
Franklin who asked the obvious question about what kind of
men "will strive for this profitable pre-eminence, through all
the bustle of cabal, the heat of contention, the infinite abuse
of parties, tearing to pieces the best of characters? It will not
be the wise and moderate, the lovers of peace and good order,
the men fittest for the trust. It will be the bold and the violent,
the men of strong passions and indefatigable activity in their
selfish pursuits. These will thrust themselves into your
Government and be your rulers."[2]

A sagacious student of human nature and political
affairs, Franklin understood the need to keep ambitious men

away from the reins of government. He even suggested the Chief Executive serve without any salary at all. He cited examples of the Quaker's community organization, and the service of George Washington as general of the revolutionary army for eight years without pay. However, many of Franklin's colleagues looked upon the idea of purely voluntary government service as somewhat absurd, given the expenses incurred by candidates.

But they may not have fully considered Franklin's concerns about elevating the motivations of office seekers, while at the same time eliminating the sheer monetary necessity for serving in public office. Franklin's theories about public service, as well as his platonic quest for the ideal republic, may seem quaint today but his concerns are by no means dead. They are even more relevant today than two centuries ago.

With a system of unlimited reelection, Franklin feared that government would degenerate into a pursuit followed only by the lovers of power and influence. To a large extent he was right. Where are the men and women "fittest for the trust?"

Madison believed that "all men having power ought to be mistrusted to a certain degree."[3] In this respect, given the troubling ethic of power, unless legislators can walk away from influence, and the other myriad enticements floating thru the halls of Congress and the Senate, they don't belong there. A passion for issues is one thing, but passion for power and elective office is another.

De Tocqueville as well cautioned against a rampant ethic of ambition in a democracy: "it is very necessary to purify, to regulate, and to proportion the feeling of ambition. We should attempt to lay down certain extreme limits, which it should never be allowed to outstep ... thus, when public employments afford the only outlet for ambition, the government necessarily meets with a permanent opposition."[4] Voters are victimized by this ambition-engendered "permanent opposition" that creates the legislative stalemates of our time.

A one-term solution would be just such a reasonable limit on political ambition. Two hundred years of transformation in our society have amply demonstrated the effects of political ambition and a reelection syndrome upon our representatives. As long as the office-holder is dependent upon the public purse for their livelihood and self-confidence and, further, must rely on special-interests for the bulk of their campaign funds, we are not likely to get fully independent representatives able to make the difficult choices demanded in today's environment. Indeed, our problems will likely multiply.

Where are the men and women who will aspire to government service without ulterior motives and warped personal agendas? And then, upon performing their period of service, leave without the maudlin pangs of personality disintegration? The fact may be we simply do not yet attract enough balanced and independent people because of the very nature of our system and society. In effect, we are all "running" for our very livelihood today.

> "Nothing is less suited to meditation than the structure of democratic society. Every one is in motion: some in quest of power, others of gain. In the midst of this continual striving of men after fortune - where is the calm to be found which is necessary for the deeper combinations of the intellect? A democratic state of society and democratic institutions keep the greater part of men in constant activity."[5]

> Alexis De Tocqueville

As De Tocqueville understood, in order to fully appreciate our present troubles we must comprehend the nature of our society and its effects upon the ordinary citizen as well as upon the political participant. There is little question we live in a fiercely competitive and striving world where we are running, literally, from kindgergarden to the day we retire, die, or drop out. There is little time for reflection and cultivation of the more graceful arts that have helped to fashion a higher level of culture in past civilizations. Our state-of-the-art toasters and microwaves should not leave us to believe that we have somehow reached a high level of civilization. On the contrary, we still have a long way to go as reflected by the current state of our political organization.

Perhaps we are plagued today by many who are fleeing into government "service" from an unsatisfactory private situation. If one's private career and sense of direction is in a shambles, one can always run for office. And to the extent that personal finances and opportunities in the private sector are less than secure our psychological hold on political office and power will tend to be distorted. Our public agenda may well be distorted by legislator's fears of return to the private sector. Among those with a fierce attachment to public office there is a powerful reluctance to give up the very position for which they may be unsuited.

Some may criticize this assumption about independence as promoting the idea that only rich people can, or should, serve in office. Certainly real independence is an attribute of character and not simply of position or sinecure. In itself, wealth does not guarantee independence of mind or great understanding. And certainly wealth is not the only basis of independence from which one resists the attraction of power in political office. But its role in permitting independence from the allure of permanent political position and government employment is not to be denied.

Of course, this is not the case with a great many men and women in public office and appointments today. Coming from successful careers, they often take a large cut in pay, and forego other opportunities, to serve. Successful people, using the more common societal definition of the word, may well be in a better position to remain unaffected by the trappings of power. But as wealth and economic security alone are no guarantee of intelligence or understanding, nevertheless, it cannot be denied they help to insulate the office holder from the worst of predations.

Ironically, if we criticize a somewhat privileged and perhaps aristocratic approach to government then, implicitly, we also criticize the framers of the Constitution, many of whom were landed gentry with time and independence on their side. In the final analysis, however, our government institutions are simply not the place to seek one's fortune at the expense of those we pretend to represent. Government "service" is an opportunity to repay, to give back, and to translate our personal good fortune into goodwill.

"AMBEGO" - A POLITICAL DISEASE —

"The desire for attention is a common affliction. And Washington is a city of epidemic ambition. It would require an encyclopedia to deal adequately with the ambego - ambition and ego - of the nation's capitol."[6]

James Deakin

Ambition and ego. In our private lives, as well as in our business or profession, such characteristics help us to achieve our goals. We need a strong ego to define ourselves fully and overcome the myriad difficulties that life presents. Ambition can be said to help us to focus and direct our goals. But the problems arise when we ask ourselves how far we are willing to go to achieve our personal goals and ambitions. If ambition alone defines our goals and methods we are unlikely to elevate the art of politics, or living. In a world where olympic athletes drug themselves to win and politicians stoop to conquer what are we saying to our children?

When we analyze objectively our ambitions and ego we begin to understand their nature and effect upon our own personalities. If a person is self-defined and confident, and pursuing their particular interests, the question of negative aspects of ego and ambition do not normally surface. What is to be gained that one doesn't already possess?

In this regard, is the desire to govern, and seek powerful political office, a manifestation of a healthy person? Why does one need to "run" to govern? And what is the true nature of the goal-driven political participant on a deeper level? What

101

is the basic attraction of political power? And what type of person now seeks "success" thru the political process?

> "I have an enormous personal ambition: I want to shift the entire planet, and I'm doing it."[7]
>
> Rep. Newt Gingrich

If we understand that it may be exactly those people who feel a need for attention and power who ultimately "run" for office, then it is easier to understand why many politicians, given the need to be reelected, will find it beyond his or her ability to withstand the temptations and trappings of power. But unbridled personal ambition is out of place in the public sector. We must change our candidate nomination and election systems to counteract the negative effects of personal ambition in our political matters. Only when the dynamite of career ambition is removed from our legislative affairs will we begin to have the quality of government envisioned by the framers of our constitution.

Those candidates who are not willing to walk away from the power and perquisites, when called upon to make the difficult decisions, are not qualified, ethically and psychologically, to be in office. A stalwart independence from outside influence, and self concerns, is the most important characteristic of the true statesman. As Madison realized, our problem in containing the worst instincts of the human animal is structural: "Ambition must be made to counteract ambition... In framing a government which is to be administered by men over men, the great difficulty lies in this: you must first enable the Government to control the governed; and in the next place oblige it to control itself."[8]

The dilemma of the body politic is how to attract, and not repel, those to elective office and government service who are not primarily motivated by the need for attention, power, money, or influence. How should an electoral system be structured to attract people to political affairs who are immune, but not deaf, to the message of our multifarious factions and special-interest groups? Under what conditions will our representatives likely be impervious to the allure of tainted campaign contributions? Will cash-starved candidates for reelection ever meet the test?

Only those who can take or leave the volatile and high profile environment of politics, and resume "real life" and their business or profession, will be likely to possess the requisite independence. But those who make a "career" of politics are less likely to voluntarily contemplate the end of the road except at an advanced age.

For the good of any republic, politics cannot be a real career, a life-long pursuit. Otherwise the trust and integrity of elective office is compromised. And politics thereby becomes a pseudo-career, one in which the participant must periodically inflate his sense of self-importance and seek the favor of others to continue his or her political profession. But what kind of independence and political backbone can the career politician maintain if making the mortgage payment depends on reelection?

Long-term political careerism ultimately engenders a sloth and deceit into our political process guaranteed to manufacture pseudo representatives - those without the courage to make the hard decisions. When difficult decisions and tough votes are called for that may serve the national interest, but possibly jeopardize one's political career, what can voters reasonably expect from a legislator with a multiple term perspective? Conflict-of-interest feeds on ambition.

> "Kind Prince, when the long age of confusion begins, people will undertake important endeavors guided only by their ambition. If he is not the slave of his ambition, he will be the slave of his emotions. If he is not the slave of his desire, he will be the slave of his ego... The forms of slavery are multiform, and may include the slavery to money, to a life of luxury, to social position, to religion, to an ideology, to the things one craves, to one's destiny, to one's biological drives, and to psychological excuses."[9]

Lao-Tzu, Tao Teh Ching

Over 2500 hundred years ago, Lao-Tzu described not only mankind but the nature of many denizens of official Washington and other centers of political power. The passage of time has not changed the truth about human beings and our seemingly immutable foibles. Although improvements in human nature may move at a glacial pace one could make a case for expecting improvement in mankind's political ethics after 25 centuries.

However, improvements in human nature will not take place in a vacuum. A nurturing environment cannot reasonably be expected to flower in a jungle of special interests, especially where cultivating one's ego and livelihood at great public and private expense is the prevailing game. Political reform and virtue need support, but not with PAC money.

> "One of absolute virtue does not need to do anything in order to be virtuous, because virtue is the very essence of one's true nature. But one of relative virtue believes that something must be done in order to prove that he is virtuous. Thus, virtue becomes prevalent when people fail to follow their own true nature." [10]

> Lao-Tzu, Tao Teh Ching

The politician's urge to "do something" and prove one's virtuosity is truly the legislator's disease. But it is a false virtue. Can we pretend that we have a better society today with our veritable mountains of legislation enacted by generations of politicians under a compulsion to justify their existence, and often their contributors enterprise? Our huge tomes of legal restrictions, largely unknown and incomprehensible to those who are expected to obey them, have not replaced the necessity of personal virtue and responsibility more easily maintained in smaller communities. Our world is seldom made a better place simply by the passage of more laws, especially in a society where "representatives" are being paid to create these very laws to protect only special-interests.

104

Indeed, as Lao-Tzu observed, criminality increases with an increase in laws. Despite our thicket of legal sanctions social expectations of probity have disappeared into ethically narrow definitions of living "within" the law. And with a rampant reelection syndrome, politically ambitious individuals will be tempted to crawl between the lines of our ethics statutes.

We have only to examine the recent antics in our Congress and Senate to find our busy representatives avoiding votes on crucial issues, especially before election time, and endulging in the folly of drafting conflicting bills so that a vote on both sides of an issue can be recorded. In addition, the urge to fill, and amend after the fact, the Congressional Record with self-serving drivel is further evidence of the true nature of the psychological fear and "sickness" that pervades our political bodies. Politicians, driven by ambition and ego, and fearful of losing their jobs, status, and power soon lose their ability to say no.

In fact, political careers are built on saying yes to every conceivable group or special-interest. We often lose the best of political candidates because they possess the rare ability to simply say no when largesse must end. But eventually all political systems, as history has amply illustrated, dissolve in excessive debt and taxes as a result of this inability to say no and the politician's willingness to carve up the public pie for special-interest banquets.

TRUTH IN POLITICS —

"They hate worst of all the man who tells them
the truth."[11]

Socrates

Too few members of Congress display the necessary political courage to deliver the truth regarding what we must do to balance our federal budgets. In fact, one must be willing to lose an election to deliver the bad news to the many constituencies who favor increased benefits from social security, medicare, welfare, public housing, defense spending, farm subsidies, public works, and the myriad other groups striving to increase their share of the public purse. But few representatives appear to display such courage, especially before or during an election? And given the circus most legislators went thru to obtain their position this fact is not surprising - their tenacity is greater than their ethics.

Consider vice-president Walter Mondale's proposal, during the 1984 elections, to raise taxes in order to balance the federal budget? Unfortunately, that very logical and reasonable suggestion sealed his political fate. In contrast, the siren song of "no new taxes" *and* "a balanced budget" proved, eight years later, to be illusory and ultimately very expensive to future generations of americans.

After Mondale, ambitious candidates have learned that a call for higher taxes, no matter how responsible or necessary, is to invite defeat. Despite the fact that we were only dealing with a 50 billion shortfall in 1984, and have since added over a trillion dollars to our national debt with yearly 200 billion deficits, voters then did not want to hear the bad news. Today, new taxes, or "revenue enhancement" as it is now called, have been stricken from the list of viable election strategies.

The lesson is clear. Candidates, coached by members of the new profession of media political consultants, will always call for the "feel-good" campaign with little reference to future obligations. Consequently, elections now generate a mass-myopia and a denial of reality. And the sad truth is we can no longer trust our candidates to tell us the truth. Evasion of the tough issues has become a "successful" campaign strategy necessitated by the nature of the reelection process. A new psychological sickness pervades our political system.

As a result, we have now had a 1988 presidential election campaign in which the major presidential candidates avoided the discussion of our federal debt problems to their seeming mutual benefit. The moral of "feel-good" campaigns is that the bad news can be delivered after the election - and only from a bipartisan commission specifically formed to protect incumbents from the wrath of the voters. This is likely to be the on-going evasive strategy of politicians who continually seek reelection. As a consequence, avoidance of issues and ad-hominen campaigns have largely replaced real debate. There are few statesmen on the political scene today.

In a recent survey researched by the New York times it was unsurprisingly revealed that, in modern American presidential elections, it was always the most optimistic of candidates who won the election. Obviously, optimism is an indispensable virtue of any leader, but good representation demands the cold appraisal and head-on look at reality. The problem voters now have is separating simple, and self-serving, optimism from truth and deliberate falsehood. Too often false optimism is simply used as a convenient evasive strategy.

There is no question, however, that the essence of the office of the President of the United States is inspirational. And good leadership is all about motivation and not necessarily management skills. The problem in recent presidential election campaigns was not necessarily one of optimism versus pessimism but simply avoidance of discussion of issues and alternatives that candidates wished to avoid and self-servingly assumed taxpayers don't want to hear. But such avoidance is definitely not leadership.

Rosy pictures of economic reality from politicians unable to balance budgets no longer cut the mustard. The fact remains that rosy pictures, and fables of a "better" tomorrow, will persist with politicians who need to get elected and reelected. The current gutting of the middle class, the de-facto devaluation of our currency, and the lowering of the living standards of Americans will likely continue until we free ourselves from this reelection syndrome. Reality does not jibe with the political rhetoric we are subjected to - and that is our problem. We must face the facts.

CANDIDATES WHO DON'T WANT THE JOB? —

"What we need is a candidate for the presidency who doesn't want the job."[12]

Andy Rooney

The basic problem with all these ambitious candidates for public office is that we don't need them. What the electorate needs are people without the driving ambition and ego to run for president for the precise reason that, once they get in office, they are less apt to become warped by it. As a society, we are plagued by politicians whose only concern is perpetuation of their own power and "leadership." When asked why he wanted to become president, John F. Kennedy candidly replied "because that's where the power is." But power is a two-edged sword, and self-interest, when carried to extremes in public life, soon warps the fabric of government.

Ultimately, the true task of a legislator is not simply to vote for every possible appropriation to benefit their district but to balance the costs and benefits over all regions. However, it is the cumulative effects of this pattern of "dog-eat-dog" political behavior that has spawned our huge budget deficits and uncontrolled spending. Able candidates and legislators must be willing to exercise independence from the selfish demands of their constituents. They cannot be bound, by oath or self-interests, to serve only the part and not the whole. One-term legislators, however, are more likely to possess the fortitude required of true statesmen to achieve lasting political balance.

A legislator's true responsibility was neatly defined by Edmund Burke upon his election to Parliament in 1775:

"Certainly, gentlemen, it ought to be the happiness and glory of the representative to live in strictest union, the closest correspondence and the most unreserved communication with his constituents. Their wishes ought to have great weight with him;

their opinions, high respect; and their business, his unremitting attention. It is his duty to sacrifice his repose, his pleasure, his satisfactions, to theirs - above all, ever, and in all cases, to prefer their interest to his own. But his unbiased opinion, his mature judgment, and his enlightened conscience, he ought not to sacrifice to you, to any man, or to any set of men living. These he does not derive from your pleasure, nor from the law and the constitution. They are a trust from Providence, for the abuse of which he is deeply answerable. Your representative owes you not his industry only, but his judgment; and he betrays, instead of serving you, if he sacrifices it to your opinion."[13]

Self-interest, reelection, and the instinct for political survival undermine real independence. Fear of loss of office is the problem. As John Steinbeck once observed: "power does not corrupt. Fear corrupts, perhaps the fear of loss of power." For multi-term incumbents, this fear of loss of power can grow with every term.

Given our human foibles, should we continue to accept a political scheme in which self-interest plays such a large role in public affairs? The federal deficit, by itself, represents the crystallized reality of the inability of congresspersons to separate duty from self-interest. It is not simply hyperbole to state that the current political system could very well bury us. We won't need war or foreign political forces to disrupt our economy and institutions. Political gridlock, created by self-serving politicians, will eventually do the same thing.

POLITICS AND POWER —

"From the nature of man we may be sure that those who have power in their hands will not give it up while they can retain it. On the contrary, we know they will always when they can rather increase it"[14]

George Mason, Virginia Delegate

109

Many professions have their problem with power seekers - people whose primary motivation is the status and influence over others that comes with position. Police academies are notorious for their attraction to sociopathic bullies wishing to continue their adolescent fantasies upon the adult population. Preachers and Priests have their obsessions with "truths." And psychologists, psychiatrists, and doctors also have their own "transference" problems and power complexes implicit in the "one-down" game of doctor and patient.

What then is the professional psychological "hazard" of being a career politician? Is it the inability not to seek reelection? Is it the inability to say no? Is "yes" so linked to self-perpetuation and reelection that management of our affairs by our representatives is all but impossible? Does the combination of special-interest campaign money, and desire for reelection, now comprise an unholy trinity with a stranglehold on our political process? Why do so few politicians appear inclined to walk away from the power and perquisites of Washington, or the home capital, and become an "ordinary" citizen? The irony is that those who willingly leave should be the ones to stay, while those who scheme to remain should leave.

Elected officials and political true believers, emeshed in their pathologically mixed mission of political and ego concerns, soon lose the ability to distinguish between personal and public interests. Some easily become over-identified with the message and the slogan, often appearing to believe no one else could possibly carry on the business of their constituents or local special-interests. The real agenda, coloring all the activities of the career politician, is all too often simply to hold onto political office. And this we mistakenly call representation.

In fact, these temptations of power eat at the vitals of even the best of men in politics. Certainly there are ethical men and women in public office today. But too many promising candidates do not enter the arena, or drop out early in the game, because of the increasingly sinister nature of the political process and their courageous unwillingness to play by the rules of special-interest politics.

> "I have never been able to conceive how any rational being could propose happiness to himself from the exercise of power over others."[15]

Thomas Jefferson

Many analysts admit the attraction to power is largely sociopathic on its face. Why then do people seek to rule, and have power over anyone other than themselves? It is not as important to understand the nature of the attraction as to realize that many are drawn like flies to centers of power and influence while others are not. However, our ability to discern the real and complex motives of people is often difficult if not impossible. And discerning the operative underlying motives of our political candidates is even more complex.

In this regard, the task of voters is formidable. But where we design, or tolerate, a system that rewards and even encourages the maintenance of personal power and influence for its own sake, via the reelection system, we are apt to attract those who are congenital power seekers and whose personal motives run stronger than any sense of allegiance to constituents or the nation as a whole. System design is thus the secret to overhauling our political institutions. A restructuring of human nature is not likely - it is reelection that must go.

> "Unless our egoic excesses are curbed by a discriminating wisdom, we run the risk of destroying ourselves. Perhaps the dilemma is a choice between ego transcendance and biological planetary death."[16]

Frances Vaughn

Given our serious world-wide environmental problems today this is not really an overstatement of the facts. We are beset by seemingly intractable problems requiring tough

111

solutions to problems created by past generations of politicians sucking from the teats of special-interests. We might even conclude that the devastating environmental consequences of the "greenhouse effect" may well be directly related to - the White House effect - a mad desire for reelection until one reaches the top.

The egos of politicians can present obstacles to difficult choices and tough, but necessary, solutions to our problems. One has only to consider the fact of multi-trillion dollar debt, and hundred billion dollar annual deficits (during a period of economic expansion no less), to realize that even Maynard Keynes is finally dead and our budget system is out of control.

But if enlightenment, or a total lack of ego-concerns, is to be a requirement for public office then it is safe to say tha not many today would appear to qualify. And even if candidates could qualify on such lofty criteria they would not be likely to run given the hoops and hurdles politicians must master. It now appears these hoops are jumped thru only by the most egoic of candidates willing to meet the un-meetable demands of public life.

Politics is the one arena where ego can wind up destroying the world. One power-bent mind on a nuclear, chemical, or biological trigger is all that is needed. And the closer to an election the more dangerous these sociopathic survival tendencies become. A cornered president still has his finger on the button of the "black box." A one-term president, however, has no such survival fantasies.

"RUNNING" FOR OFFICE —

> "Good men are not willing to rule for money or for honour - for they are not place-hunters. Therefore constraint must be put upon them, and a penalty if they are willing to rule, and that is really why it has come to be thought an ugly thing to present yourself willingly for office and not to wait for constraint. For in fact if a city of good men could be, they would fight to avoid ruling,

112

just as they fight now to rule; and then it would become quite manifest that indeed a true ruler's nature is to look for the subject's advantage, not his own."[17]

Socrates

Could Socrates view our political arena today he would undoubtedly agree that we are plagued with a legion of "place-hunters" and office seekers. The process of self-nomination, frequent elections, and the all too attractive perquisites of power combine to breed the ambitious politician.

What motivates candidates today? And what does "running" accomplish for the candidate or the voters? Our candidates are literally running themselves to death in silly and frantic manueuvers to "meet the people" and engage in any number of non-essential media-events. And, in the case of incumbents, instead of doing their job and attending to the business of serving their own constituents they are "running" for an office, which in most cases, they already hold! When election fever strikes, most incumbents have a hard time sitting still.

In the age of television and satellite communications this silly perpetual movement and campaigning is no longer necessary. Our political candidates are busy polluting the atmosphere with jet fuel, and the airwaves with bombast, while they ignore the very jobs for which we pay them. This self-serving activity, to the extent it is carried on today, is grounds for impeachment from their present positions. Instead, due in large part to this excessive campaigning, we reward them with another term despite the time and money they have wasted to convince us of their own righteousness! Our votes are being bought with our own money and legislative time.

So much taxpayer's time today is wasted by representatives in thinly disguised personal campaign efforts unrelated to the business at hand. It is safe to say that these same people, employed by private business, would be summarily fired for the same investment of time in personal affairs while on company time. The truth is voters would do well to "fire" many of our representatives for their galling and egregious misuse of the taxpayer's time and money while they are busy preparing for reelection. There is little question the electorate is tired of candidates running for office who seem incapable of avoiding the "promise-this, promise-that" mentality of candidates on the make.

The very word "running" suggests the desperate pull of ambition, and fear of loss of influence, that attracts the wrong crowd to the game. The term also accurately captures the senseless mad-cap pace of modern day political affairs. If candidates simply "sat" for office, in a subdued and shortened process of debate before a bipartisan appointive body, or the larger body politic via television, we could eliminate the circus atmosphere of politics as we know it today.

It is this very carnival along with the demeaning demands of campaigning and fund-raising that repels many decent and capable men and women who might otherwise consider service in government. Today, many would agree that the system eliminates more worthy candidates to public office than it attracts. Can we get the legislators we need thru our present election apparatus, or do we presently keep them from being available for holding office? Will the qualified candidates who win elections be able to maintain the highest of ethical standards and avoid conflicts of interest in today's money-grubbing political environment?

It is no secret that candidates who openly express their independence and unwillingness to cater to special-interests simply don't last in the real world. Such fortitude is not an asset and is punishable by loss of campaign funds. The strong and independent cannot succeed. Special-interests support those candidates who will commit, regardless of future circumstances, to a pre-conceived position in exchange for money. Thus, the voters are left with these "winners."

Simply put, the statesmen's dilemma is that in order to qualify for office, with a higher standard of ethics and morality, one must not seek power in the first place. This is the essence of Socrate's formula and Ben Franklin's argument about political service. Both questioned whether we can have "elections" in which people "run" for office at all? I think they are right. We would have better government if all, or a greater number of our representatives were first nominated and then appointed by a qualified bipartisan body of people who represented the diverse interests of the community? In this way the "runners" might be kept out of the race.

POLITICAL VERTIGO - THE STRESS OF CAMPAIGNING

> "You know, there were times during the campaign when not only didn't I know where I was, I didn't know who I was."[18]

> Hubert Humphrey

> * * *

> "There is nothing worse or more damaging to a normal, healthy family life than either the father or mother being involved in politics."[19]

> Frank Lutz

In recent years we have witnessed numerous candidates on the ragged edge of exhaustion and mental instability as a result of this process of "running" for office. Is a "survival of the fittest" mentality the only process and criteria we can devise for selection of our elected officials? Who survives?

The process of "running" for office is debilitating to our candidates. Psychologist, Lynda Towle Moss, likened the process and its effect upon the candidate to that of cult conditioning and emotional breakdown: "when you keep a person up all night, isolate them from their families and all that's familiar, and keep them busy 12 to 15 hours at a time, it breaks them down emotionally."[20] In other words, politics today can be dangerous to your health, your family's health, and the health of the body politic.

One can also argue that the process of campaigning itself distorts the candidates perspective and contributes to an ego problem and ability to weigh the issues fairly. A "successful" candidate can develop a misplaced sense of omnipotence and power that may, in fact, have had more to do with the dislike of his opponent. Ultimately, the results of the campaign process itself can be harmful to the candidate's mental state in the process of governing. Add to this the near inability to lose, once an incumbent, and you have the makings of political megalomania.

Journalist Cathy Lawhon observed that: "Politicians - and anyone else who gets caught up in an ego game such as campaigning - begin to think: We know best. We have the best ideas. We can deal with issues better than anyone else. Soon, the process has got you instead of you having it."[21] It is not an exaggeration to state that such unnecessary travail leads inevitably to real polarization and stalemates in our legislative processes. The winners come off with an "attitude" that does little to advance solutions to our common problems.

Still others argue voters get the benefit of a candidate able to withstand all the rigors of running the political gauntlet. We must ask, however, what character of candidates desire to endure this questionable process? And, at the end of a long race, do we merely get athletic and strong, but otherwise dull and vapid, candidates willing to engage in such questionable marathons? Can we not say the senselessness of the activities required to run this political gauntlet are totally unneccessary and must be reformed?

Consider the length of the presidential primary process, now complicated by more states competing to have ever earlier primaries than others, and how this has extended the presidential political marathon to absurd lengths. The more than a year long process of campaigning has little or nothing to do with governing or the development of insight into any particular problem. In fact, it contributes to partisan squabbling and detracts from the very process of governing. In the process, the majesty of the office is greatly diminshed.

Without question political campaigns today have become a serious waste of time, money, and energy. Surely we have entered the age of the video-phone and satellite hookups that eliminate the necessity of continuous travel for politicians as well as legions of staff and reporters who participate in, and lend credence to, these unreal events. The process of campaigning now has more to do with raising money, for more campaigning, than it has to do with issues and good government. Campaigning breeds more campaigning, ad infinitum.

The reality of campaign activity today is that many elected officials are playing hookey from their jobs and neglecting the duties of office. This is particularly true where the candidate is running for an office other than the one he presently holds. In this situation, the representative's constituents are clearly getting shortchanged.

In our modern political arena there is good reason to believe we can no longer persuade the best and the brightest to seek office - the personal costs are too high. In this respect, it may be said that our campaign system winnows out more winners than losers. The truth is the geniune statesmen of our era may accept appointment to high positions but getting these same outstanding individuals to "run" for office today is entirely another matter.

"TYPE-A" POLITICS —

"People coming into government from private life are shocked at the compulsive intensity and the workaholic ethic of Washington, of Congress or high in the Executive branch."[22]

Hedrick Smith

Many observers of the Washington scene have lamented the toll the "Type-A" capitol life-style takes on our politicians and government officials. The inevitable result is often more family tension, higher divorce rates, and nervous breakdowns. As Hedrick Smith pointed out: "Washington has one of the highest number of psychiatrists per capita in the country, testimony that workaholism and the pressure-cooker atmosphere of Washington life are an occupational hazard." Can we accept that this is an atmosphere likely to produce optimum government? Far from it.

Do workaholism and good government mix? Is the growth of bureaucracy simply the long-term result of an overabundance of compulsive and driven "type A" overachievers? Are politicians, with the notable exception of President Reagan, simply afraid to take a more relaxed view of public management? In view of the fact that we have no accepted measure of political productivity other than that of producing more legislation, and much of that at the behest of lobbyists and special-interests, how do we judge the "productivity" of our government?

Job stress, and the "hollow superficiality" of the cocktail circuit, drains the vital juices out of our politicians. Like the lobbyists they have become, legislators swim in a sea of "contacts" with overloaded agenda's allowing little time if any for a private life and such frivolous things as intimacy and friendships. "Busyness" itself has become a problem as Chris Matthews, aide to former House Speaker Tip O'Neill observed: "The problem with Washington is it's all an imput town. You can't measure outputs, you measure imput. This is a town where the GNP is government. Government is measured not by output but by how many hours you put in. Everybody says, 'I've been really busy this week.' Are you busy? I've been busy. I must be busy. And it's like busy-ness is a value in itself."[23]

Smith's analysis of the deleterious effects of capital politics and the busy "power game" on political participants is, indirectly, an indictment of the multiple-term, career-oriented, politician. We now place our representatives into situations that effectively guarantee only the "best" of the power players will survive - and to what end?

> "The quest for power and the relentless pace derive
> from a deep inner feeling of inadequacy and
> dissatisfaction that breeds loneliness... There is
> an addictive quality to all this... you've always got
> to go one higher. The politician never really trusts

as much as one would imagine. So much is bled out of them in constituency demands, in legislative demands, in family demands that they wind up after a number of years saying, 'What's left of me? Who am I?' "[24]

Dr. Steven Pieczenik

In a world where every meeting and function must have a purpose the agenda is usually permeated by the desire for power and influence. But this compulsive competitiveness and goal driven behavior empty the real life from our representatives. The obsessive fear of defeat and loss of power diminishes the human being. Endless campaigning and fund raising seem to leave little time for governing and attending to the affairs for which they were elected. With one eye on the polls, politicians speak carefully crafted and prepared positions for different audiences - spontaneity is avoided like the plague. Thus, there is often little of the real person that emerges in the packaged candidate until after the election. Are we governed by shrunken beings?

Voters and the media are also participants in this type-A madness when we tend to punish legislators, like Ed Muskie, for displaying human tears in public. Real men it seems show no emotion. But do voters want "real men" in office or do they prefer the well-scripted competitors for whom any display of weakness is anathema? It seems we prefer to create our own political Frankensteins.

CHAPTER IV

— CAREERS AND CORRUPTION —

CAREER BUREAUCRACY & CIVIL SERVICE REFORM

"Our constitutional form of government, with three separate but equal branches, has now been radically changed with the growth of the federal bureaucracy, a fourth branch of government more powerful than the three others. This unelected bureaucracy, which has the power to create regulations with the force of law, presents a serious threat to the freedoms of all American people. Today's civil service system was designed to prevent the abuses of the so-called spoils system. The Civil Service Commission, however, has become a spoils system of its own. Its hiring and firing practices virtually guarantee a job to anyone who passes the first year of probation. With severe limitations on changing the policies of the bureaucracy due to the antiquated civil service laws, the expedient reaction is no reform at all."[1]

Sen. Dan Quayle

In addition to the defects in our electoral system, good government is stymied by the careerist nature of civil service. The federal government now consumes over 30 per cent of our Gross National Product as compared to less than 10 per cent in 1930. A work force of more than three million civil service workers now spend literally trillions of dollars annually on thousands of programs. Approximately one of out six americans works for the federal government today as compared with one of every 204 in 1935. And regulations totalling nearly 1.5 million pages have been posted in the Federal Register since 1940 alone.

It is clear that Congress and the Executive branch must soon regain control over the federal bureaucracy if we are ever to solve our budget problems. With thousands of agencies able to promulgate rules and regulations affecting our freedom, and with virtually no oversight by the elected representatives charged with legislative responsibilities, bureaucracy now has a free rein. As Senator Quayle stated: "There are so many rules and regulations that an accurate count is virtually impossible; yet, every American is responsible for knowing and complying with these laws. Every president since Herbert Hoover, recognizing a good campaign issue, has pledged to reduce the bureaucracy. But, without exception, each one has not only failed but has seen government grow during their term of office. The growth has been wild. While the population has increased 60 times since the founding of the republic, the size of the bureaucracy has now increased 8,170 times."[2]

In other words, since our founding as a nation, the size of the bureaucratic state has increased well over 100 times as fast as the population. There is no rational explanation for this except to explain it in terms of a virus.

Certainly we have legitimate need for government functions. But the advent of the modern civil service has locked us into a system that grows by inertia and feeds on the dwindling reserves of the taxpayer. Commenting on our bureaucracy and admistrative despotism over a century ago, De Tocqueville observed that excessive government "covers the surface of society with a network of small complicated rules, minute and uniform, through which the most original minds and the most energetic characters cannot penetrate."[3] Amen.

The problem of bureaucratic growth in the United States stems from a lack of presidential control and appoitive power over the federal bureaucracy. Very few federal employees are now under the president's management jurisdiction. Less than 1 per cent of federal employees are currently subject to elimination or replacement by the president. Thus much of government is immune from our own elected Chief Executive! The will of the bureaucracy, survival being its basic agenda, has become supreme over that of our elected representatives. This must change.

> "Why are the people starving and leading a difficult life...? Because their rulers consume too much tax grain - That is why they are starving and leading a difficult life."[4]

Lao Tzu, Tao Teh Ching

Lao-Tzu's ancient observation illustrates how little things change and how simple is true wisdom. But politicians love to make our problems appear more complicated than they are. We often hear the phrase that there are "no simple solutions" from the very people without the backbone or political integrity to attempt any solutions whatsoever. The fact is our problems often are simple - the problem is that effective solutions are likely to hurt re-electable politicians.

Generations of "experts" and consultants have thrived on government funding and spreading the self-serving belief that our problems are intractable and require decades of expensive study. Further "study" of our problems is often just political code for the inability of legislators to face the issue prior to an election. And more delays, prompted by frequent elections, work to further aggravate the serious problems at hand, in spite of the fact that we normally know intuitively, if not factually, the proper response to the issue in question.

To obtain effective solutions to serious issues, without delays due to political considerations, will require a new breed of citizen-legislators free of ties to special-interests and designs on reelection. Otherwise, every major issue paralyzing our legislatures will have to be solved by initiatives, requiring direct popular vote and bypassing ineffective representatives.

Another major reform area that will require tremendous political backbone or, in the alternative, a national initiative, is the reform of the federal pension system. At all levels of government pension costs are now taking an increasingly large part of the operating budgets. In the case of the federal government, combined pension outlays now total well over 20% of the budget. Despite efforts to reduce the COLA's, or cost of living adjustments, to meet Graham-Rudman deficit targets, the surge goes on in spite of the fact that 75% of Federal retirees collect indexed social security and indexed civil service pensions.[5] This is in stark contrast to the fact that very few workers in private industry have any automatic cost-of-living wage adjustments.

In the case of large municipalities like the city of Los Angeles, for example, pension costs absorb over 70% of the annual operating budget! In other words, career politicians and bureaucrats have staked out an alarmingly high proportion of our tax revenues for their own interests.

It should come as no surprise to discover there are many present and former members of the Congress and Senate who are double, triple, and even quadruple-dippers - or multiple pension recipients. In other words, we pay them for the past, the present, and the future all at the same time! And many of these politicians are among the approximately 350,000 federal retirees whose pension payments now exceed the wages they once worked for.

Growing federal, state, and municipal pension costs are a danger to our economic well-being as taxpayers. In 1983, at the federal level, of the 39.4 billion received by the civil-service retirement system to fund future benefits, 55 percent came from the taxpayers, 33 per cent from income earned on the fund's investments, and only 12 percent from employees![6] As with Social Security, the pension system is, in large part, a ponzi scheme pushing the real costs onto future generations of taxpayers.

At one time there may have been a measurable difference from private sector payscales for many government employees to warrant extra benefit treatment. However, this is clearly no longer the case, and taxpayers are now stuck with excessively high personnel and pension costs. Whatever the solution, there is no question that future Presidents, Congressmen and Senators will be forced to raise federal employee pension contributions, and reduce benefits, if we are ever to balance the budget. Here again, this may well be a task requiring the fortitude and independence of single-term representatives.

Multi-term politicians and career bureaucrats have made pension funding a disaster, and have given new meaning to the term "gravy train." However, with a single-term service ethic in government, I believe we can not only attract the best and the brightest, but also at the least cost over the long haul. Huge public pension benefits do not need to vest for those whose private plans are intact and can be resumed upon return to private life. And for those who enter public life with sufficient assets to disavow interest in public pensions, the term "public service" will have even more meaning.

Surely if public employment today were particularly onerous or unfair then we could expect to see a high "quit-rate." But the opposite is just the case, the quit-rate of our government employees is well below the average for private industry.

Along with solutions to problems of political corruption, and conflict-of-interest in elective office, we must continue to reduce the bureaucratic gravy train. But one is not likely to occur without the other. In the absence of strong congressional and senatorial representatives the political will to reform and streamline our federal agencies will be missing. As it stands today, many politicians up for reelection utilize the services of career bureaucrats in a mutual back-scratching relationship that ensures the political survival of all parties. Thus long-term incumbency turns our representatives into bureaucrats.

The one-term solution is one approach to ending the on-going relationship between bureaucrats and incumbents who put their personal priorities above the will and good of the people. Reform of the civil service, and placing appointment and review powers over a broader spectrum of bureaucratic posts into the hands of elected officials and bipartisan committees, will give the people greater control over their government.

CAREERISM - GOVERNMENT AGAINST THE PEOPLE?

"We want to create separation of powers... but do we want to create a class of professional politicians?[7]

Sergei Plehanov

A new generation of Soviet party officials today are taking a fresh look at the effects of their rigid government and party structure. They are now seeking reform and looking for ways to provide for separation of powers, and checks and balances, while also avoiding the bane of "professional politicians." Decades of decay and one-party political corruption have led to a monumental stagnation of the soviet economy and political process.

Premier Gorbachev's "perestrioka" restructuring efforts are no less than a call for total reform of soviet politics. The new reforms include freedom for new political parties to emerge and challenge the stranglehold of the bureaucratic monster created by the Communist party. The Russian people have witnessed, with depressing clarity, the ultimate effects of careerism and party stagnation. Still, there is doubt whether Gorbachev's attack on bureaucracy and career party officials will ultimately be successful. Similarly, in the United States, we have also developed a de-facto system of near permanent incumbency leading to our own generation of professional politicians, election paralysis, and political stalemate. A minister of the Kremlin Secretariat once complained that one couldn't do business with the United States because we are always having an election! And there is truth in this statement because we do have unending campaigns and constant electioneering. As a consequence, important matters, like arms reduction and world peace, are continually put on hold.

Whatever the political system, it is slowly perverted by the meshing of personal ambition and political position. When the interests of elected officials and government employees run counter to the interests of the people, how good can government be? The public is the odd man out in this incestuous political relationship between industry and government insiders. Truly independent legislators, omsbudsman, whistle-blowers, and public activists are all anathema to the well-laid plans of government insiders.

The nature of tenured employment tends to produce lifetime government employees estranged from the common private sector activities of the majority of citizens. Thus, a bureaucrat's perspective will tend toward the monolithic and paternal, perhaps due to never having been on the other side, the private sector, in their careers. In effect, an us vs. them mentality pervades many government departments created by a tenured association of individuals dedicated to self-perpetuation at government expense, and always at the service of candidates for office who present no threat to their survival.

This insularity, bred by careerism and life-time employment in government, can and does develop into outright hostility toward the private sector. Of course, this is not to say that it is not government's legitimate function to protect us from the worst of private-sector predators. But a senseless adversarial hostility is often reflected in the stifling flow of bureaucratic regulation that chokes our systems of commerce, communication, and transportation.

It has been heard from more than one president they have been looked upon by career heads of federal departments as short-term nuisances, to be held at bay until another hapless president is brought in who may be more easily cowed by powerful capital bureaucrats. In this fashion the dynamic of career public service often works to the detriment of the people's interests. Bureaucratic power is seemingly impervious to change or disruption by such minor elected officials as the President of the United States.

Generally speaking, careerism in government leads to the public's concerns being continually subordinated in devious ways to the office holder's interests. And over time our government apparatus has become arthritic and vericose, its veins filled with the cholesterol of money, fame, and ambition and tenure. Career civil servants, and continually reelected politicians, form a natural back-scratching sludge that clogs the arteries of our geriatric government. Unless the body politic exercises its right to unclog the system the nation will continue to suffer a slow strangulation.

Recognizing the existence and influence of our entrenched bureaucracy is vital to our understanding, in any meaningful fashion, of the incestuous modern day relationships between powerful institutions both public and private. This great body of government simply did not exist in the late eighteenth centruy when the framers deliberated the wisest approach to electing, and re-electing, representatives. Our remedies, short of serious reform, are slim - we cannot impeach or easily dismiss errant federal employees. Truly effective management of our government will require independent and powerful agency heads as well as the elimination of tenure.

TENURE VS. MERIT —

The tenure system of career employment must eventually be revised before taxpayers, or our representatives, can expect to regain control of government agencies. Merit and need must return to play a role in staffing agencies responsible for public spending.

The original rational for tenure in government, like that given to teachers, was low pay in relation to the private sector. And where government payscales were indeed measurably lower the lure of long term job security supposedly made up the difference. For taxpayers concerned with quality government, however, the unanswered question is whether the sacrifice in flexibility of management of our agencies is worth the price. And what quality of personnel is engendered by such a pay ethic? Do we actually save any money with lower payscales or simply induce a rigid oversupply of less than qualified personnel while, at the same time, not providing proper incentives to attract the best of talent to government service.

The ethic of "government bashing" prevailing during the Reagan era has not served to solve our problems. In fact, it has likely multiplied our problems. The truth is that we will not attract quality people to government while such service is held in low esteem and payscales are significantly less than the private sector. Nor will we attract the best where government places of employment are best described as "drab and dingy." With tenure, and sub-standard working and pay conditions, we are locking ourselves into inferior civil service performance with no possibility of change by creative and independent management personnel. Short of eliminating tenure, streamlining management, and improving working conditions and salaries, how can we expect better government?

A recent study by the Hudson Institute, a conservative "think tank" reiterated these very themes and stated that our government's "ability to recruit and retain the best" has now severely deteriorated.[8] The Reagan era, while initiating some needed changes, has, in effect, helped to depress the morale and initiative of federal employees and leave taxpayers with a slowly growing "crisis of competence" in government. Unfortunately, the often well earned disdain of the average voter for the antics of professional politicians sometimes, undeservedly, carries over to all other branches of government service.

The very atmosphere of government employment must be changed. There are too many "needless aggravations" associated with public employment. Limited advancement opportunities, poor working conditions, random drug testing even for those who are not suspected of drug use, and the practice of monitoring phone calls all combine to create a nightmarish "Big Brother" mentality and environment surrounding our civil service. What talented person, with options in the private sector, would opt for work under these conditions? We will never repair and rejuvenate our civil service until we attend to these basic work conditions.

But change must start at the top - we cannot revitalize the ethic of government employment without renewing the ethics of our representatives. Short of a one term solution, will Congress ever stop attempting to significantly increase its own pay, thru commissions designed to issue pay increase recommendations only after elections? The latest proposal to increase congressional salaries is $135,000 per year, up from $89,500, along with a $26,000 honorium ceiling! Of course, the salary alone does not take into consideration pension benefits, staff and office perquisites, junkets, and use of reelection PAC-money, etc. The proposed increase alone, of $45,500 per year, is nearly equal to the "dream salary" of $50,000 annually sought by the vast majority of working americans!

The Hudson study pointed out that our federal workers, on average, earn 24 per cent less than their private sector counterparts.[9] But this disparity is even greater in the higher ranking jobs where salaries in the private sector may reach several multiples of what government has to offer. In the higher positions, we clearly need adjustment to more commensurate levels of pay, with that of the private sector, if we are ever to attract the best of management talent and streamline government.

But does tenure alone "fix" this disparity of wages? By itself, tenure does not offset the inferior salary, atmosphere, and working conditions that repel the best and the brightest from civil service. In many cases tenure simply locks in the least capable and efficient into important government posts and thereby prevents contructive change. Simply put, the tenure system has not benefitted taxpayers. In place of our tenure system must come a limitation of term for many posts. More federal positions should be limited along the lines of the fifteen-year term given the Comptroller General of the General Accounting Office, or the fourteen-year term of a Federal Reserve Board Governor. Longer appointments are rightfully designed to de-politicize these posts and place certain key officials well beyond the sway of elected officials.

In the event of single-term legislators, however, even these terms may be too long and counterproductive. More 4 to 6 year bipartisan appointments would be appropriate for many departmental posts. This same shorter-term appointment approach should be taken with a wider group of federal administrative positions. We need more medium-term management appointments, by bipartisan commissions, to avoid party consciousness. In this way the cancerous effect of tenure and party allegiance can be diminished.

But simply raising civil service wages while, at the same time leaving tenure untouched, would be another costly mistake. There is good reason to believe that civil service could be changed and improved by negotiating higher wages, on the short term, for elimination of tenure and certain pension benefits. The taxpayers need a quid-pro-quo. The voters, their elected representatives and appointed department heads, need the ability to radically reform and streamline our mammoth bureacratic state.

The ideal of "service" in government has been buried under the reality of tenure. Instead, we have created a large body of employees, whose wages and generous pensions are paid by the taxpayers, and whose long-term interests run counter to that of the electorate. The important question is what caliber of people, with tenure aspirations paramount, are we attracting to career government "management" thru excessive benefits as opposed to the basic wage and intrinsic satisfactions of a non-tenured short-term appointment?

Realistically, those with fewer options in the private sector will be the most tenacious office holders, as well as the most self-serving politicians and bureaucrats, in the long run. Power complexes, and fear of unemployment, only grow with length of term in office. It is likely we breed a careerist mentality in government employees and politicians with too ample benefits and too many years of service. While I am not advocating that we pay less than a decent wage, still, those who see holding public office and agency appointments as primarily salary and benefits are not the type of people we need in public office or the top management of our government agencies.

With tenure, and the byzantine nature of qualifying for a government post, we have prevented the emergence of a one-term bureaucrat. As opposed to merely seeking elective office for one's stint of government service, there are many agencies where short term management appointments could serve to add energy and new ideas to management. A large part of our political problems stem from the fact that we have now turned government service into a career, an honorarium into a wage, and a noble calling into a job. And for men and women of talent, the compensation of government pay will likely never equal their "worth" in the private sector. Should government pay necessarily attempt to equal that worth? I don't think so. This is a necessity only for those lower level positions where job activities and requirements differ so little from the private sector.

There is "worth" to maintaining a stable and responsible democracy? A dollar value cannot be placed on "service" in government, especially in a one-term environment. In response to the "call" of public service, many appointees and political aspirants with substantial personal fortunes willingly deposit their assets into blind trusts and enter public life free from possible conflicts of interest. Government is indeed enriched by the willingness of "successful" people to set aside private affairs and contribute to the administration of public affairs. We must encourage more such participation to give birth to a successful one-term revolution.

Of course, whether one has substantial means is not the issue. A "means test" is not appropriate for government employment or public office. We must begin to re-embellish the non-financial rewards of government service so those of high ethics, independent spirit, and good character can feel drawn to public service, regardless of financial status. But first the appearance, and actuality, of corruption and influence peddling in politics must be eliminated.

Problems with tenure and careerism plague our government at all levels. People who come to Washington as legislators, staff, or consultants, tend to stay on either by wrangling a post with another agency or becoming a lobbyist. Too many choose never to leave the circles of power. And the reason may well be that they no longer have any business, or interests, or even home to which to return. For this reason, our career politicians, lobbyists, and bureaucrats are involved in a backscratching relationship that only strenthens the sub-government. In effect, we have a built-in conflict of interest in our bureaucracy - the interests of government "servants" versus the taxpayers.

Some may contend that a one-term solution is a revolving door approach to government. In one sense, this may be true. But our very problem has been the rigid *unrevolving* nature of representation today. In this sense, the very strength of the plan is the elimination of careerism. And there is likely to be another important benefit. With limited terms, single-term candidates for office, or government employment, are more likely to come from an established background, having achieved a degree of security and currency in their profession or industry. We will draw from a greater pool of talent.

Are we wise to continue to fill the capitals of political power with people whose entire resumes are filled with political jobs? Is "expertise" the disease?

To improve government we must defuse the virus of careerism and tenure. Given the potential for abuse, we can safely say participation in government should not be a legitimate career. We all come from the private sector and we must all return. The administration of the public sector does not require a class of permanent plutocrats, or government eunuchs, divorced from the difficulties of private pursuits. Government service is simply a revolving necessity, a time when one must serve their "watch" with the interests of all at heart.

However, the re-emergence of such a patriotic service ethic will only occur when careerism is eliminated from government.

SUB-GOVERNMENT" -INVISIBLE POWER

> "Sub-government is self-perpetuating and endures over a long period of time, unaffected by the tides of opinion and efforts for reform. It is made up of spokesman for the largest corporations, specialized law firms and a bar association, the trade press, trade associations, public relations and management consulting firms, and various other hangers-on ... It also includes the permanent government staff - regulatory, executive and congressional - which is concerned with day-to-day activities of the private interests in question. People in this sub-government typically spend their entire lives moving from one organization to another in the sub-government. People who pursue the course of protecting the public interest are rarely admitted to this club."[10]

> Nicholas Johnson

The "revolving door" between regulators and the regulated has often given us only the illusion of industry oversight. A "Sub-Government" described by former FCC Commissioner, Nicholas Johnson, remains in firm control today.

Where the interests of career government employees and legislators become so suffused with the people's legitimate business we have a recipe for producing unnecessary self-serving ventures at the nation's expense. Our unwieldy buraucracy today is the tired result of rampant careerism and self-proliferating departments that spawn their own needs and defenses against elimination. Over time the bureaucracy and sub-government have effectively divided and conquered the body politic due to their influence with re-electable, district-tied, congressional representatives.

And the efforts of government reformers are often undercut by careerists. The Grace Commission, on government waste, is perhaps a good example of this phenomenoa. In this instance, thousands of specific remedies and solutions to government waste and inefficiency were proposed by the commission, headed by industrialist J. Peter Grace. But few, if any, were adopted. Efficiency and consolidation, as opposed to growth and expansion, are seldom on the agenda of government agencies.

On the other hand, in a rough and tumble free enterprise economy we need effective government oversight as well as the threat of substantial penalties for private-sector misuse of the public trust and taxpayer's money. The Reagan years, however, have resulted not only in an explosion of useless weaponry but a gutting of anti-trust and environmental programs ultimately leading to a higher cost, and lower quality, of living for all americans. In these instances the legitimate missions of the agencies in question were overtly throttled by ideologue agency heads. The result has been more serious pollution and more oligarchy and an ultimately self-defeating concentration of wealth. The pendulum has swung too far.

The legitimate mission of federal oversight agencies is effectively subverted by the sheer force and influence of the sub-government. Regulatory agencies must be staffed by people of integrity and vigor able to withstand the powerful forces of major industrial corporations. But when these same staff people often come from the very corporations they must now police, and to which they may return, what can we expect? The revolving door must be closed.

With regard to our reform proposals, what would be the likely interaction between one-term legislators vis-a-vis the entrenched bureaucracy? Will they be able to cope? Will they be able to streamline government? If we change the terms of office for our congresspersons, senators, and president, how will this affect the balance of power between our elected officials and unelected bureaucrats? Would career civil service employees in our state and federal departments acquire even more power in relation to more transient single-term representatives? Would an overhaul of civil service also be necessary to consider the one-term alternative?

The increased independence of single-term legislators would increase our chances of streamlining bureaucracy. One-termers could take the heat of dismantling bureaucracy and sub-goverment profiteering at taxpayer's expense. Only legislators without the need to seek reelection funds, and thus committing to protecting the "pork" interests of the local constituency, can be expected to tame the bureaucratic monster. The plain truth is that no generation of re-electable politicians has ever been effective in controlling the costs of government, or offsetting the power of the sub-government. And none will.

THE BEST DEFENSE PORK BARREL CAN BUY —

"The self-interested politics and economics of many parties, the armed services, Congress, the president, the defense industry, and large segments of the american public - intrude into almost every aspect of a weapon's conception, development, manufacture, and deployment. When these special interests assert themselves - through the democratic process or on its margins - the results are predictable: billions are wasted on weapons deployed at strategically impractical locations, a defense strategy that lacks coherence, and mindless acceleration of the arms race. After a continuous 40-year defense buildup, marked by such repeated excesses, the military program is totally out of control."[11]

Nick Kotz

To understand the true impact of the defense establishment, as well as our sub-government, we have only to consider the Pentagon with its massive budget equal to that of the total GNP of the top 100 New York stock Exchange companies! The combined effect of the pentagon's political influence and largesse in each congressional district is enormous. Even the most budget-minded of careerist representatives soon become great advocates of local defense pork-barrel.

The Pentagon's huge impact on the economy and the average American community is substantial. Almost without exception, every state and community in the nation have an "interest" in defense spending. The funding of installations and procurement of weapons systems pervades our economy like no other single industry. The pressures on congressmen and senators to lobby for continued funding of defense programs in their state, however outmoded, is fierce.

Thus the cumulative effect of fifty states feeding at the pentagon's trough is colossal waste and mismanagement as well as a tragic waste of our economic power. What is "good" for the local communities is, in toto, disastrous for the nation as a whole. In this environment defense spending corruption, fraud, and waste have been largely ignored by legislators who fear the wrath of the sub-government. Defense largesse is akin to easy drug money, once you get used to it it's hard to stop.

Eisenhower's famous warning to "beware of the military-industrial complex" was not enough to stem the enormous tide of wasteful defense spending since the end of WWII. It is highly unlikely we will ever "disarm" and streamline our own defense establishment with congressmen and senators subject to continual reelection and obligatory pledges of support for local defense contracts. Under our present election system, our representatives simply cannot be counted on to take the measures necessary to re-establish real civilian control over the military and curb wasteful spending. Peace is unlikely to break out of this stranglehold.

Today, it is increasingly evident that our real wars are economic and not military. But our economy is still perverted by the war mentality. And with a military budget six times that of the Japanese and West Germans (as a percentage of GNP), we have subsidized our own economic destruction with our absurd levels of expenditures in useless and outmoded military programs. Almost five decades after the end of WWII we still have hundreds of thousands of troops stationed around the world wasting obscene amounts of money maintaining out of date protection committments. And all in an era when cargo troop planes can be anywhere in the world within 24 hours! In addition we continue to build billion dollar planes and battleships that can be sunk with a $5,000 missile - a strategy so effectively demonstrated in the Faulklands war. In short, our defense strategy is bankrupt.

Congressional legislators are mandated by our constitution to control the national purse and manage our financial affairs while responsibly providing for the needs of the republic. The truth is that congressmen seldom see it that way.

> "Pork-barreling has gotten a bad name. That's what
> I'm here for. It turns out to be one of the few
> tangible things we can do in Congress."[12]

Rep. Douglas Bosco

This is a catastrophic mentality. Our federal government is now spending over one trillion dollars annually - a sum that just a few years ago would have seemed recklessly imposssible. The average congressman perceives his or her primary duty and responsibility to first and foremost get as large a slice of the federal pie as possible to benefit their constituents. And getting a better than "fair share" of the federal "Pork barrel" is perceived as the essence of the job. And the justification for these expenditures is secondary, especially given the fact the majority of weaponry proposals are generated, not by the military, but by the large defense contractors.

Thus diminishing the overall size of the defense pie is rarely considered. Overriding duty and responsibility to the nation, in toto, is given only lip service but little real concern by our congressional representatives. We simply must find a way to re-orient the priorities of our congressmen or our republic will collapse via a cruel inflation brought about by this pork-barreling mentality. But how will voters rearrange the priorities of our representatives when with every reelection comes the promise of more largesse? Reelection itself breeds more pork!

> "The pork barrel affects virtually every decision that Congress makes. Defense spending, for example, is now a larger slice of the hog than public works, and when the Defense appropriations bill is brought to the floor, the bitter fights that occur are not over strategy or policy, but between members who represent airplane manufacturers in California and those who represent airplane manufacturers in New York or Missouri. This not only costs Americans dearly in their pocketbooks, but in our national security. So pork-barrel has become not only wasteful but dangerous. And that is why it must be brought under control."[13]

> Rep. Jim Weaver

The full effects of the pork-barrel mentality and process were well outlined by William ashforth: "the pork-barrel system figures heavily in the problem of congressional favoritism toward special-interests; interferes with the orderly activities of the great federal agencies and politicizes agency decisions; promotes interdistrict and interstate rivalries where enlightened self-interest would call for unity; has caused massive environmental damage like drying up the Everglades, pouring salinated waters into Mexico and Canada, and filling in fifty-one valleys in Mississippi and Alabama with soil dug from a canal being built because barge companies convinced a few powerful congressmen that the current route is too long."[14]

In recent history only presidents Eisenhower and Carter have had the guts to veto public-works bills. Eisenhower's veto was overridden by Congress, but Carter had better luck in finally eliminating some of the lard. Today most such public-works projects are funded almost entirely by the federal government. Eventually, it was President Carter who suggested some form of "cost-sharing" where local government would be required to pay part of the costs of federal projects of primary benefit to a small area.

This simple and effective approach would also alert local taxpayers to the shenanigans of their "representative" and the influence of local special-interests. However, the truth is that when it comes to our own backyards voters selfishly want all the pork they can get. This is precisely why we need to restructure and eliminate the effect of this local bias on the sum total of federal spending.

The "line-item veto" power sought by many presidents is another device that might impale pork projects in their infancy. However, as now required the president must either sign, or veto, the entire text of each bill precisely as presented by Congress. Opponents of line-item vetos contend that it turns the President into a dictator and destroys the separation of powers intended by the framers. However, the president is the only elected figure with a national constituency! The president's district is the nation. Every other elected official is responsible to a part, but not the whole - and therein lies the problem.

We have not even begun to see a rational use of our defense dollars. And we are kidding ourselves if we think that we can continue with the present character of our political system and be successful in cutting wasteful military spending.

LAWYERS ON TOP OF LAWYERS —

"The special information which lawyers derive from their studies insures them a separate rank in society, and they constitute a sort of privileged body... This notion of their superiority perpetually recurs to them in the practice of their profession. Some of the tastes and the habits of the aristocracy may consequently be discovered in the characters of lawyers. They participate in the same instinctive love of order and formalities; and they entertain the same repugnance to the actions of the multitude, and the same secret contempt of the government of the people. The government of democracy is thus more favorable to the political power of lawyers; for when the wealthy, the noble, and the prince are excluded from the government, the lawyers take possession of it... They fill the legislative assemblies. The lawyers of the United States form a party which is but little feared and scarcely perceived... but this party extends over the whole community, and penetrates into all the classes which compose it; it acts upon the country imperceptibly, but finally fashions it to suit its own purposes."[15]

Alexis De Tocqueville

If only Alexis could see us now. Today, the Lawyers Party is in full control of our political institutions. And we need only to examine the makeup of our legislatures to get a feel for the unrepresentative nature of our representatives. The vast majority of legislatures simply do not reflect the makeup of our society. They are filled with lawyers and career politicians who represent only a tiny fraction of the diversity available. In this respect, former Rep. Richard Bolling observed, in 1963, that 406 members of Congress, out of a total of 435, listed "politics and civil service" as their background. In addition, 249 members of this group were lawyers.[16] This narrow professional grouping is typical of our legislatures today.

But where are the dentists and the doctors? Where are the architects and the teachers? Where are the small businessmen and women? Where are the real estate entrepreneurs and corporate moguls? Where are the self-taught blue collar philosophers? The real question posed by the nature of our lopsided legislative constituencies is whether legislatures so skewed with people from one profession can pretend to fully "represent" the diversity of the american people or, more pointedly, avoid conflicts in legislation designed to further interests of their own profession - namely litigation. As former Chief Justice Charles Evans Hughes so aptly stated: "The United States is the greatest law factory the world has ever known."[17]

The ordinary citizen, to a certain degree, is locked out by this professional stranglehold on our legislatures. But there is little reason for the average voter to feel intimidated because the process of good government is certainly not a mystery requiring a priesthood schooled in arcane jargon. The framers themselves were not career politicians and bureaucrats with positions to protect. Good government is simply one part common sense and one part courage. It is also knowing when not to act. And it is produced by people with experience in all walks of life acting in concert. Our government should not be so dependent on a priestly class of lawyers whose very occupation depends on the adversarial obfuscation of basic issues leading to inevitable litigation and paralysis.

In a larger sense, the manufacturing economy of the United States appears to be on the brink of sinking because so few today want to produce tangible items anymore, especially with domestic labor. We have bought the "service economy" myth. And despite a devalued dollar our manufacturing base is largely being abandoned and moved to cheaper labor markets. Our massive and unrelenting trade deficit is partly a reflection of the fact the best and the brightest of today's young people are atttracted to largely unproductive pursuits pushing paper and influence in stock manipulations and legal battles in a vast zero-sum shell game. And many more are engaged in useless tax manipulation schemes, deriving from a byzantine tax-code, put together by legislators under the influence of special-interests at election time. It is doubtful we will ever solve our balance of trade problems with hordes of talented people who persist in producing nothing but a blizzard of paper, influence, lawsuits, and media puffs.

However, with creative change from a new generation of one-term legislators, we could begin to dismantle the surplus legions of lawyers and accountants whose energies might be put to better use and function in our society. Recent letters to a popular business journal prove the point: "Sir: I have made my living from complicated income tax laws for more than a dozen years now. If a simpler tax law is ever passed, well,

I'll just have to find honest work."[18] Another letter revealed the utter depths reached with recent tax legislation: "Sir: The current tax law was drafted and passed by a Congress that does not understand it. It was signed by a President who does not understand it. And it is interpreted and enforced by the IRS, which publicly admits at least 25% of its personnel are unable to answer taxpayers inquiries accurately. Such tax law is not merely poor law or bad law, but despicably rotten law and accurately reflects the total contempt Congress has for the ordinary American citizen."[19]

Our bloated modern thicket of laws, or "verbal jungles" as they were appropriately termed by semanticist S.I. Hayakawa, are gradually strangling every sector of life and commerce. And any "simplification" will remain a dream as long as self-interested professionals rule the roost.

> "The more corrupt the state, the more numerous
> the laws."[20]

> Tacitus

Consider the 1200 bills passed by the California State Legislature in the last two weeks of the 1988 term! Over 3700 bills were passed in all. The truth is that legislators don't even read, much less debate, the majority of bills emanating from the on-going legislative special-interest onslaught. The process has become a farce. However, one editorial writer suggested a novel solution: "Reduce the incentive for lawmaking by limiting the number of terms a politician can serve and require that for every new law written, two old ones be replaced."[21] Not so farfetched.

All these legislative proposals always sound good despite their true intentions and effects, masked on their face as they often are in unarguable and politically potent themes of apple-pie and motherhood, patriotism, or "saving" taxpayers money, etc. But that is the lobbyist's art: "making all the right sounds to cover the noise of money leaving the taxpayers' pockets."[22] Even legislators have a hard time discerning who is truly benefiting from many of these laws. But in the "I'll vote for yours, if you'll vote for mine" atmosphere of most legislatures the career backscratch prevails.

The over-professionalization of our economy and political institutions today is evident in the regulations emanating from our legislative bodies. Incomprehensible legislation, often spiked with special-interest exemptions and riders, is the only product of those whose career interests are tied to deciphering and litigating the very legislation they produce. What happens when lawyers write the laws, when accountants write the tax code, and polluters write the pollution statutes? We are living with the results of such a system. We can do better - we could hardly do worse.

PEDDLING INFLUENCE —

Shortly after the influence-peddling scandal involving a former Reagan aide, the Senate passed a bill dubbed the "Never again Mike Deaver Bill." The intent was to tighten the screws of post-employment restrictions on Executive branch officials. The spectacle of thousands of government employees eagerly trading on their public positions, to enhance their return to private life, was finally capped by the Deaver affair.

The purpose of the bill is to prevent out-going officials and representatives from any paid lobbying of Congress, or top administration officials, for a period of at least one year after leaving office. The hope is that this reform will prevent the "cashing-in" mentality from running amock amongst former public officials. Congress, however, has yet to pass a similar bill.

But as is the case with much "reform" legislation there tend to be "sleeper" provisions that make a mockery of the stated intent of the bill. In this regard, journalist Stephen Chapman pointed to the way incumbents cripple their opponents under the guise of reform: "The Same bill extending the ethics laws to Congress harbors a provision strengthening the incumbent preservation laws, otherwise known as campaign finance reform. It forbids those elected to Congress to raise funds after the election to repay personal loans to campaigns. This prohibition won't hurt many members of Congress seeking reelection since their position makes it easy for them to raise funds before the election."[23] It is challengers that are severely restricted by this provision.

By drawing our future representatives from a greater pool of private-sector professionals, instead of the same revolving group of career politicians, we may prevent government officials and elected representatives from trading on their position and influence in the private sector. And those with only lobbyist backgrounds and influence peddling to look forward to, after stints of government service or elective office, may be more easily spotted by the voting public with a knowledge of where their representatives are coming from and where they are likely to return.

It used to be that people came to serve in Washington, or their state capitols, and upon a change of administration or the end of their term, simply returned to their community. Now the trend is different. According to "headhunters" in the capital, at least 70 percent of officials and staff today are choosing to remain in the centers of power chiefly for the reason that they have little or nothing to return to and seek to enhance their private positions by trading off their government service. And so the army of lobbyists and consultants grows wildly, leading to increased power and influence for the sub-government class.

With only "politics and civil service" in one's resume to fall back upon, what degree of independence is likely to be exercised by the preponderence of legislators in this situation? Can career politicians, with a vested interest in maintaining their position, bring the requisite degree of independence to the job? Many would say not. And "reform" legislation emanating from Congress makes the case even more eloquently.

It all points to the fact that we need to close, or at least slow down, the "revolving door" between government and private industry where influence is one's only product. The growth of lobbyists and influence peddlers in our political system has given rise to a new sub-class of de-facto officials who, while temporarily out of office or position, nevertheless make their living trading on their former government service - Washington D.C. has become an economy and world unto itself.

We are more likely to recover the nobility of politics and government service with single-term reforms encouraging greater participation by a larger segment of the population. It is no accident that "politics" has become a dirty word. It need not be. Single term elected officials may properly pass the baton to their successors and move on in their personal lives, or even to an appropriate higher appointment or office given the vote of the people. For the long-term health of the republic, however, the reelection treadmill must be brought to a halt and politics revitalized with single-term citizen-politicians.

PATRONAGE POWER & APPOINTMENTS —

"Trouble begins when party officials are given the patronage power over particular agencies."[24]

Ronald Goldstock

Patronage and nepotism, or the giving of favors and positions to friends and relatives, is one of the oldest of political abuses. This type of political corruption tends to occur most often at the state and municipal levels, where corruption and influence occur over long periods of time and become accepted as the "way to do business." Again, the main problem is prolonged incumbency. Combined with the perquisites of patronage, political power can become a powerful narcotic. Elected officials begin to believe the political territory is their own fiefdom, one that is only inconveniently subject to periodic reaffirmations by an apathetic and misinformed public.

It is no secret that ambassadorships to "prestige" posts have often been up for "sale" in past presidential campaigns. Major contributors received a promised qui-pro-quo in the form of particular appointments. In these instances, we have turned important ambassadorial posts into ceremonial plums of patronage that were "sold" to the highest bidder. In the process, we often short-changed our allies.

Certainly the citizens of the host country are insulted by such appointments when it is evident merit did not enter into the ambassadorial decision. And the morale of qualified candidates suffers in these instances when high profile ambassadorships become toy jobs for multimillionaires and their wives who dream of fancy ball gowns and lavish state dinners. But such is the stuffing of patronage.

In recent years we have seen many abuses of the appointive power, especially from the White House. But certain appointments are simply too critical to be left to elected officials. For example, political power may become excessively entrenched when presidents and governors have appointive power over strategic offices, such as the Attorney General. Often this crucial post goes to one of the most trusted cronies - witness a Bobby Kennedy, an Ed Mitchell or Ed Meese. Justice was not done in these appointments.

Especially in the case of the Attorney General, close advisors cannot reasonably be expected to serve the interests of the people against the candidate should the need arise. The conflict of interests and loyalties is self-evident and yet we accept it. Why do voters allow this unsatisfactory structural situation, and appointive power abuse, to continue to exist? Where are the "checks and balances" in this arrangement? Where was the "advice and consent?"

We must restructure the people's access to these crucial appointments so that our top elected officials are not protected *from* the people. Restructuring appointments, and placing more critical positions into the hands of bipartisan bodies, rather than our elected officials, is one way voters can regain control and recapture the integrity of government. We, the people, are subjected to the worst of political hacks simply because of an outdated tradition. This must change. Elected officials must be disarmed going into office and they're hired guns left at the door.

147

However, as long as we continue to ignore the psychological traps built into our run-for-office political system, we should not be surprised at the continuing failure of mere human beings to serve the public interest. We get the kind of government we deserve as long as we organize the system the way it is. And if we continue to be mesmerized by tradition, and narcotized by our incumbent's media messages, the voting public will not consider alternatives. Until we examine what is, we cannot imagine what could be. If we cannot imagine what it could be, then we cannot summon the will to change the system and reaffirm the contitutional power given us by our forefathers.

CHAPTER V

— "WE, THE PEOPLE" —

NEW POLITICAL PARTIES? —

"The only remedy is to enlarge the sphere, thereby dividing the community into so great a number of interests and parties that in the first place a majority will not be likely at the same moment to have a common interest separate from that of the whole or of the minority; and in the second place, that in case they should have such an interest, they may not be apt to unite in the pursuit of it."[1]

James Madison

Much like an economy where little or no competition only produces monopoly and overpriced goods, a political economy may suffer from the same problems where few parties and a limited spectrum of political goods exist for the voters. Politically speaking, the United States is starving.

Madison believed that, if parties must exist at all, then a large number of political parties and factions worked best to secure the interests of the body politic as a whole. With a plentiful choice of parties voters were less subject to influence by one tyrannical majority, plurality, or party. His vision of multiple parties and factions was a good deal more democratic than our present two-party affair, however raucous such a reality might be.

Why have we not seen the emergence of a major new party, of any significant size, in the last hundred years? What is it about our current political system that discourages, or prevents, the rise of new and alternative parties? Why have we fossilized into a two-party system when other parliamentary democracies have spawned a wider, and more vibrant, political spectrum?

Could it be due in part to the sad fact that, of some 28 democracies in the world, only Columbia ranks below the United States in voter participation?[2] Or is it simply the result of the stranglehold of our two major parties on the media and the electorate? Whatever the reason, the traditional Republican and Democratic parties today function largely as vehicles for the reelection of incumbents. They are obsolete except for the fact that, in practice, no one can be elected to office today without first going thru these hoary political organizations.

While I am not suggesting that a country, like Italy, with its manifold parties and constantly reforming governments (whose modern post-war average lifespan is approximately ten months) has demonstrated any particular expertise in democratic reform, my point is merely to illustrate the rigid nature of present day American politics with its two-party system and a seemingly unstoppable ascendency of the incumbent.

Few would question the proposition that americans suffer from a lack of diversity and independence in our political parties and representatives. And if two parties are better than one, what are we to say about three or more? Recent reform in Mexico addressed this problem of sterile two-party monopoly by expanding the Chamber of Deputies to 500 seats, and permanently reserving 150 seats for minority parties.[3] The full spectrum of political opinion in a democracy cannot function without such provision for wider representation. We have no such inclusive provision in the United States.

Perhaps a more relevant question today is whether we even need political parties? Would the voters be better off with more bipartisan nominating organizations? Are parties simply an albatross around the candidate's neck? Are party platforms meaningful or do they just hamstring candidates and cater to special-interests? The truth is the major parties have simply become fund raising devices manipulated by self-serving politicians with little loyalty to party platforms once in office?

And voters in any democracy worthy of the name should not be compelled, by the dominance of the two major parties, to continue to pick our leaders from amongst those who already hold office, and whose entire career may consist of one political bid after another. But because of the very power of incumbency today this is exactly the problem. The public's choice of candidates is vastly narrowed by the traditional process so well mastered by incumbents. The current system confines politics to career politicians, or multi-millionaires, with the money to put them on an even footing with incumbents. This is not the political system envisioned by the framers.

Although our two-party system has now become stale and increasingly irrelevant to many voters, the major parties still control the nominating process and play a big role in deciding who will ultimately get to run. Third-party candidates and independents today are virtual non-entities. It is a political tragedy that we, in the United States, have only two parties thru which it is realistically possible to elect a president. This political monopoly, firmly in control of the nomination process, effectively closes the door to all but incumbent politicians and party insiders - the voters have few options.

The barriers and expense of third-party formation are too great today to allow those of a more independent mind to seek office thru any other regime than that of the Republican or Democratic parties. We are left with a two-party funnel of mediocrity thru which we process individuals and wind up with the most compromised candidate. Only candidates with the necessary special-interest campaign financing, and who are thus potentially obligated to protect the status quo, can make it thru the funnel. However, once incumbency and campaign financing problems are removed, new parties and independent candidates will flourish and democracy will come alive. Today "minor" parties such as the American Independent party, Libertarian Party, New Alliance Party, Peace And Freedom Party, etc. are virtual non-entities. Getting past the intentionally crippling "threshold" requirements to garner a foothold, financing, and media attention necessary to mount a sustained campaign is a formidable task for new parties. The political deck is stacked in favor of the status quo.

A two-party monopoly is our problem and not the solution. But changes in our nominating procedures, campaign finance laws, and media time-sharing rules could change this dismal state of affairs and enliven our political environment.

Despite its origins the United States today is not a very dynamic political culture. Compared to the range of discussion and debate in other democratic countries, American political debate is narrow and vapid. This peculiar parochialism has, at times, been very evident to others. De Tocqueville, a keen observer of the American character, noted the post-revolutionary beginnings of our strange sheepish tendencies in 1835:

> "I know of no country in which there is so little independence of minds and freedom of discussion as in America. In any constitutional state in Europe, every sort of religious and political theory may be freely preached and disseminated. In America, the majority raises formidable barriers around the liberty of opinion. The Empire of the Majority succeeds much better in the United States. If ever the free institutions of America are destroyed, that event may be attributed to the omnipotence of the majority."[4]

Alexis De Tocqueville

The problem with two-party monopoly and winner-take-all type politics is that it effectively eliminates the opposition. And where majorities rule, minorities wail. When the majority is in the wrong, or changes its collective mind, the tide is slow to turn due to the almost complete absence and disarray of any opposition. Thus an "Empire of the Majority" and two-party political monopoly create barriers to creative change. And, more importantly, the existence of only two major parties serves to intimidate independent candidates, sans party, from entering the arena. The electorate cannot be properly nourished on such a limited political pablum.

Why not more parties? Why is there a two-party hegemony and stranglehold on our electoral process? Could a third, or fourth, party today get media coverage of its convention? The odds are slim. The fact is we have locked ourselves into a two-party scenario despite its increasing irrelevance to most of the voters. The scandal of the 1988 elections is that two minor parties, Libertarian and the New Alliance Party, have achieved ballot status in 45 or more states and yet remain literally invisible to the voters due to media neglect.[5] They are caught in the Catch-22 of modern politics: not being perceived by the media as big enough to effect the outcome of the two party monopoly and yet having no chance of doing so without such coverage.

The voters are cheated by this situation. How big do new ideas, and candidates, have to be? The sad reality is that big parties, big media, and "big" incumbent politicians combine to monopolize our political arena and frustrate any attempts at alternatives. In the long run, however, the broadcasters, architects of this neglect of our true political resources, are simply setting the stage for license review and mandatory air time requirements prompted by irate voters.

With regard to the two party dance, it can be said that the history of all "civilized" cultures is but a litany of struggling groups and factions. Whether rich vs. poor, farmer vs. merchant, debtor vs. creditor, patrician vs. plebian, labor vs. capitol, or religion vs. religion the followers of one group or another are destined to smoother the rights of the other once in power. The same dualistic dynamic of revolving oppression, with little progress in between, characterizes the ebb and flow of power from one faction, or party, to another.

And where politics remains so neatly defined into either-or categories, and two-party structures, society will continuously lurch from one viewpoint to another. The loser in this political dynamic is any notion of "progress." In effect, there is only continuing polarization and seldom real coalition and resolution to issues under such circumstances. Elimination of parties or, at the very least, a greater number and diversity of political clubs where no single party constitutes or claims a majority, is more apt to facilitate coalition and compromise.

Over time our two-party system has successfully deadened the political instincts of an increasing number of voters. From active political participation by the voters of the original thirteen colonies, we have lumbered forward into a great political sleep. It is time to open our political, and media, arena to a greater array of parties and independent camdidates. When access to political debate is effectively closed by the media, to those not currently in office or belonging to the major parties, we all lose - and democracy suffers.

"COMMON COUNCILS" & BIPARTISAN NOMINATIONS

"All combinations and associations, under whatever plausible character, with the real design to direct, control, counteract, or awe the regular deliberation and action of the constituted authorities, are... of fatal tendency. They serve to put, in the place of the delegated will of the nation, the will of a party; and according to the alternate triumphs of different parties, to make the public administration the mirror of the ill-concerted and incongruous projects of faction, rather than the organ of consistent and wholesome plans digested by common councils, and modified by mutual interests."[6]

George Washington

* * *

"The American system was surely meant to have a possibility, at least, of the people operating directly on their government, without any party standing between the people and the government and compromising or bartering or simplifying their wishes - pursuing the aims of the party at the expense of the aims of the people."[7]

Charles Mee

It was the intention of the framers to protect our flegling nation from the influence of political parties. As Washington stated in his farewell address, the very efficacy of "common councils" is defeated by the party mentality.

Shortly after the Constitutional Convention, parties began to emerge along the urban-rural divisions between merchant and farmer. As Richard Hofstadter relates, the federalists denounced these new organizations as subversive. They declared that "the representative institutions of republicanism were in themselves sufficient as instruments of government, and any attempt to set up political clubs or societies outside them would be an attempt not to extend but to destroy republican institutions."[8]

Charles Mee pointed to the efforts made by the framers to insulate our original "electors" from political influence: "The electors would meet in their own states, not gather at some central place - which would prevent them from getting together in a cabal and bargaining and plotting for their own interests, the way modern parties do. Political parties are, in the operation of the ideal republic, to be viewed with suspicion."[9] Only the unsullied and uninfluenced process of electing electors, from common councils, could guarantee the popular will was done in the election to the highest office in the land. In short, our system was designed to work without political parties.

In a single-term political system the process of nomination becomes even more important. There won't be a need for parties per se, only "common councils" or bipartisan nominating bodies. And how will qualified candidates make their appearance? Or get nominated? And how do we prevent a multitude of special-interest influence peddlers from crowding the field? How will pre-eminent and unaffiliated persons of merit emerge in the midst of our present two-party system run by party professionals? The answer is they can't, or won't, unless such a system of bipartisan merit nomination replaces "running" for office.

For a one-term process to work, the nominating process is clearly in need of reform. Currently, the party process is guaranteed to produce the "safe" candidate from amongst a stable of long-term incumbents. Such persons may simply be the most compromised and PAC-financed individuals of the bunch, and exactly the wrong persons for the job.

More bipartisan nominating committees must be formed, at various political levels, to produce the names of qualified and interested individuals for elective office as well as others to serve as "electors" to other nominating levels. The voters deserve a wider field of candidates from which to select their representatives. We need to open up our nominating process, encourage new parties, widen debate, and free ourselves from the two-party hydra strangling real political democracy.

In the era of telegenic "maverick" candidates the influence of a party upon voters is declining while the sway of personality and special-interests is increasing. Political scientists have noted for decades the diminishing pull of parties in the media age. We've become a nation of individualists rather than party loyalists, but party structures still control media politics and the nomination process. In fact, we have yet to exercise the freedom potential of the information age.

Since americans no longer appear to blindly follow the lead of the major parties, voters routinely split ballots today. This "breakdown" of party discipline also carries over to legislators. As Representative Thomas Foley observed: "nobody in the Congress ever talks about the Democratic or Republican party. I have never heard a member of the Congress refer to a colleague and urge a vote for him because he was in the same party. Most Democrats and Republicans could not recall three items on the platform of their party... We have 535 parties in the house."[10] Another representative put it more succinctly: "you can look around the floor of the house and see a handful - twenty years ago, you saw a lot of them - today you can see just a handful of hacks that were put there by the party organization, and there are very, very few of them left. It is just mostly people who went out and took the election."[11]

The crux of a potential candidate's dilemma today is that before they can make their positions known to the public, they must have met the "qualifications" of special interests and big contributors to get into the game. Unfortunately, for the electorate the unaffiliated, unknown, unpledged, uncompromised, and unmortgaged individual is not in the race today - and this is our problem.

> "Until an effective legal control of the causus system shall be devised, and the civil service reformed, the only remedy at hand for the evils of the caucus system is a greater amount of what has been described as 'individuality in politics.' Public opinion may in this country never permit self-nominations to elective officers, but in smaller districts, at least, very much may be accomplished by spontaneous or independent nominations, made by a few well known men of high character, which shall claim popular support not because they pretend to be made by a majority of the party, but because they are intrinsically excellent, and are certified to be so by the men of recognized reputation who make them."[12]

> Frederick Whitridge

Over a century ago Frederick Whitridge pointed to the main problems with party politics, namely the dearth of good men who would put up with party hoopla to seek office. Primary elections were the remedy for the evils of the back-room caucus system and Tammany Hall-type politics. Unfortunately, the caucus, or town meeting, method of nominating candidates was eventually usurped by powerful factions and parties and grew into a systematic procedure of denying those outside party structures access to the nomination process - hence the proverbial "smoke-filled rooms." And what was once a vital process of citizen participation was gradually monopolized by party professionals and incumbents.

John Adams once stated that "our revolution was effected by caucus, the Federal constitution was formed by caucus, and the Federal administration sustained by it."[13] In other words, our democracy was born in a caucus. It is also important to remember that the function of caucauses in early American politics was to pick an "elector" or person who would vote for the president in an "electoral college." Electors would then travel to the capitol, take the pulse of the candidates, and vote accordingly. It worked for awhile.

Today, the primary is our caucus. But it retains little of the flavor or spirit of participation of the real thing. Those who do not belong to a major party, or who may be registered as independents, cannot vote in primaries organized and controlled by the two major parties. Party insiders still dictate, to a large extent, what and who the vast majority of voters will have the option of deciding they are for or against. "None of the above" is not yet a political option. In fact, the concept of a plurality, or election to office with less than a majority, becomes a necessity because we so rarely see candidates who can inspire and motivate a true majority.

However, less than a century after the revolution, our caucuses had already been subverted by their very size. Limits in caucus size were necessary to retain any individuality and relationship to the community. In 1895, George Layton suggested that three hundred people, perhaps organized around the local school district, was the only workable representative affair possible. Electors should come from these small neighborhood bodies. Democracy could then be a true trickle-up process and not merely a rigged game of special-interest nominees gaining the imprimatur of the people via television commercials.

"Avoid large assemblies." This was Layton's prescription for a successful caucus. The essence of democracy, according to Layton, required that we "do not bring the electors of a large and populous district into one caucus. Increase the number of caucuses by assigning so small a territory to its jurisdiction that the number of all the electors within it will not be too great for every resident to be known by sight to his fellows."[14]

Layton's final prescription for serious political reform was the need for civic participation: "If 'good' men would maintain self-respect by properly performing their share of political work, at the time and place the 'bad' perform theirs, and which they perform so effectively as to cause the former to complain of them, the dawn of the political millennium would soon appear above the horizon."[15] In other words, we cannot leave the field of politics to career politicians.

The basic truth is that small neighborhood and community caucuses are the invisible threads of democracy that unite a legislature and bind their trust. If we believe in a republic, as opposed to a media controlled democracy, then the re-emergence of a new neighborhood caucus system is the place to start. And unless we involve ourselves in our communities we become simply at-large citizens with no local roots and responsibilities.

The question of self-nominees, versus caucus and party nominees, is an interesting one. Surely we must have a system where it is possible for persons of merit to appear and either declare their candidacy or be nominated on merit. With "merit" drafts of suitable prospects, regardless of previous party affiliation or loyalty, we can then pick the best candidates.

> "Gentlemen and fellow citizens, I presume you all
> know who I am - I am humble Abraham Lincoln.
> I have been solicited by my friends to become a
> candidate for the legislature. My politics are short
> and sweet, like the old woman's dance. I am in
> favor of the internal-improvement system and a
> high protective tariff. Those are my sentiments and

> my political principles. If elected I shall be
> thankful, if not it will be all the same."[16]

Abraham Lincoln

Simple and sweet. In his first attempt at public office, Lincoln presented his credentials in the best fashion. Despite these "humble" beginnnings, however, Lincoln lost his first race but later, thru the caucus system, become the nominee and was elected.

In contrast to Lincoln's self-effacing approach, careerist self-nominees today often reek of ambition and ego. Voters have had their fill of candidates, a la Richard Nixon, whose entire political career was one interminable run for the presidency. Unfortunately, the boyhood dream became our nightmare. Instead, let us design a system in which more men and women can surface from the great reservoir of talent in America, and where neither wealth, nor previous party affiliation, will have any bearing on the voter's ability to choose the best candidate.

ELECTORAL COLLEGE OR ELECTRONIC LEGISLATURES?

> "The executive should be independent for his continuance in office on all but the people themselves. He might otherwise be tempted to sacrifice his duty to his complaisance for those whose favor was necessary to the duration of his official consequence. This advantage will also be secured, by making his re-election to depend on a special body of representatives, deputed by the society for the single purpose of making the important choice."[17]

Alexander Hamilton

* * *

"The United States shall guarantee to every state in this union a republican form of government."[18]

Article IV, Sec. 4, U.S. Constitution

* * *

"The electoral college method of electing a President of the United States is archaic, undemocratic, complex, ambiguous, indirect, and dangerous."[19]

American Bar Association

Is direct electronic democracy somehow outlawed by our constitution? Has technology rendered quaint our charter and the institution of the Electoral College? Is a representative, or republican form of government so favored by the framers now outmoded and a relic of the era of horse-drawn carriages? Has technology permanently altered the meaning, and effect, of our constitution?

In the original design of the Electoral College system every effort was made to prevent political cabal, intrigue, and corruption in electing a national president. The framers did not look with favor upon the institution of a popularly elected president. For the most part, they feared direct democracy and the power of the people. In fact, in the early days of our republic, democracy was a dirty word.

From the framers perspective, this small body of Electors "deputed" by the people, and cloistered away from the wiles of campaign rhetoric, would gather and make a rational choice in the best interests of the nation. Regardless of the results of the ballot process, electors may not necessarily be bound by the majority vote of their constituents. Indeed, the votes of the electors has, at times, gone against the popular vote.

To understand why we have such a college, and not a direct vote for president, it is necessary to understand how much the writers of the constitution feared "the french contagion" or mobocracy. The essence of the electoral college system was that it would act as a buffer against rampant democracy and a catering to the mob for political favors. Thus, the electoral college may very well owe its existence to the impact upon the framers of the excesses of the French Revolution which began the same year the American Constitution went into effect in 1789.

The college was to serve as protection against the people's presumed inability to deter demogogues from office. Ironically, it was thought necessary to protect the nation from its people and not the people from the nation. In this sense, the college is an aristocratic device - a "fail-safe" political mechanism to preserve the status quo and give a few electors the power to actually reverse the will of the electorate. Also, we would do well to remember the framers had no idea how long the newly formed United States would last. There was no guarantee the constitution would not be overturned by even the first president of the new confederacy. Thus, the framers, reflecting an aristocratic and republican bias, wanted some insurance and back door control over the people power as well as the presidential power - enter the electoral college.

And to insure the integrity of the College no senator, representative, or person holding "a place of trust or profit" under the United States could be amongst the electors. In this respect, the electoral college was intended to be a distilled body of "the people" whose judgment would somehow be less tainted and superior to a simple majority of the voters, or to an assembly of politicians subject to manipulation by their fellows. In addition, the electors were to assemble and vote in the states in which they were chosen, and not mix en masse where political turmoil and corruption might take place.

The college functions in presidential elections when the registered voters cast their ballots, not for the candidates directly, but for slates of electors "pledged" to a particular candidate and drawn up by the political parties in each state. State election officials then tally the popular vote and all electors of the slate that have received the most votes are then certified as duly elected. In December, after the November vote, official electors meet in each state and cast separate ballots for President and Vice-President. Depending on state laws, some electors are free to vote for whomever they please. But being quasi-political party officials, electors almost invariably vote for the party candidates favored by the voters.

The votes of each state's electoral college are then sent to Washington where they are counted by tellers appointed by the House and Senate. The results are then announced, by the president of the Senate, in a joint session of the new Congress on January 6th. If a presidential and vice-presidential candidate received a majority of the electoral votes, they are deemed elected. If not, the President is then chosen by the House of Representatives and the Vice President is chosen by the Senate.

But what might happen today if the College did not ratify the popular vote? As William Syre and Judith Parris pointed out in their study of the college, in fifteen times out of thirty seven, a candidate who had not received a majority of the popular vote was declared a winner by the electoral vote. But even this estimate is difficult since counting of the popular vote did not always take place (only electors votes counted). Essentially, a "runner-up" president can be elected by winning many small states and losing by a slim margin in those states with big blocs of electoral votes. This is why our modern presidential races have become electoral-vote bidding wars with candidates courting certain states while ignoring others.

However, in a one-man/one-vote world the electoral college, in all its republican glory, has become a fiction. It is now a mere relic of another political era. And due to technology the ideal of a one-man/one-vote world is more nearly a reality today than ever before. But that ideal is subject to party politics. About the only function the college serves today, aside from making it possible for other than a popularly elected candidate to win the election, is to also guarantee that a winner will be a standard-bearer of either of the two major political parties. Independent and third-party candiates, bypassing party apparatus and emerging from the electronic media jungle, might have trouble getting past the all but defunct electoral college. But would the people's will be done?

Ironically, our nascent electronic media democracy has the potential today to simply become an enlarged electoral college where voters, as enfranchised electors, can simply cast their ballots in their own homes or locals. The principle is the same - only the number of electors is changed. Electronic democracy promises to open up a whole new world of political participation. Our twentieth century ability to interact electronically, without the device of electors, has undermined much of the original rational for the system. And if we can elect electronically, we can also impeach electronically. There is no longer time and distance between us and our representatives - everything and everywhere exists in an electronic now.

But if one views the modern electorate, the broad middle class, as "rabble" then perhaps there is still justification for a device such as the electoral college. However, if we do not accept such a premise we should be prepared to accept the reality of "electronic democracy."

The primary problem with the college is that electoral votes are not proportional to popular votes. Each state has as many electors as the state has senators plus representatives. In general, the state's entire share of electors is awarded to the party receiving a plurality of that state's popular vote. This "winner-take-all" approach is very effective in eliminating any representation for minority parties and independent candidates.

The tyranny of the majority leads to the tyranny of the two-party system and their slates of electors. Because state laws vary widely regarding the eligibility of minority parties and independent candidates, the electoral college is a system that is seriously out of balance. Since the Civil War, minority party candidates have managed to win electoral votes in only five presidential races. As Alexander Heard wrote, "Third parties in America are doomed so long as our present contitutional arrangements are maintained."[22]

The call for reform of the electoral college has been nearly continuous since the first "faithless" elector, in 1796, bolted the party, followed his conscience rather than his pledge, and voted for the "better man."[23] Thus, the realization there may well be a discrepancy between the popular vote and the electoral vote has since promoted numerous reform efforts. At present, the president is elected not only under rules set by the constitution as well as federal and state laws, but also by political party rules that carry out the mandate. But exactly what each person is voting for, in a national election, varies from state to state. Ballots and rules for candidates, as well as electors, vary considerably. This lack of uniformity in rules and regulations amongst the states, regarding the people's vote for a national executive, makes a mockery of the institution.

One alternative, a "direct-Vote" plan, offered as an amendment to the constitution, was debated and approved by the House in 1969 subject to a ratification which never took place. The plan counters some of the obvious defects of the electoral college.[24] Basically, the pair of persons receiving the greatest number of votes for President and Vice-President would be elected, provided they obtained at least 40% of the vote, or otherwise there would be a run-off election. This plan would also open the system to new parties and candidates, perceived by some as "spoilers" who might complicate the politics of a run-off election in attempts to extract concessions from leading candidates.

The advantage to the voters, in increasing the number of eligible candidates and thus their overall choice, is not to be discounted. The direct-vote plan might well encourage many more last-minute candidacies based on lackluster poll showings of party-candidates. This could be a blessing to the voters and the nation. However, those who oppose a direct-vote plan seem to feel that voters should not have this open ballot option. Rather they should remain obligated to choose from amongst major party candidates who may well have manuevered their way thru to the nomination due to incumbent advantages and overly plentiful PAC financing. Worse yet, major party candidates are apt to feel they are owed the presidency regardless of what voters would have prefered were they given a real choice at election time. The "mandates" are bogus.

The District plan, introduced by Sen. Karl Mundt in 1969, was aimed at eliminating the winner-take-all approach that awards all of a state's electoral votes to plurality winning candidates. It also seeks to establish electoral areas not unlike our current congressional districts.[25] Each state would have two senatorial, at-large, electors and more according to equally-sized districts drawn by the states themselves. This plan would tend to offset the advantages currently enjoyed by the more populous states and destroy their ability to aggregate electors votes and "pledge" themselves to eager candidates. For example, in 1968, California recorded 40 electoral votes for Richard Nixon. But under a district plan, that same vote would likely have given 23 votes to Nixon and 17 to Hubert Humphrey - a much more democratic result.

On the other hand, smaller states, with two senatorial electors, would tend to acquire more leverage and increase the chances of a "runner-up" winning the electoral vote over the popular vote. And in a rapibly urbanizing world the influence of the smaller states would appreciate over time and disenfranchise urban areas. The problem with a district plan is that districts tend to be so large that cries of gerrymandering or unfairness always emerge. One solution would be to make districts so small (neighborhoods, for example) and numerous that such squabbles do not arise. And as districts decrease in size the problems of fairness begin to disappear, but so too does the rational for the college itself. At some point, districts as well should be dropped in favor of a direct popular vote.

Like most reform legislation, proposed changes to the electoral college system have been sidetracked due to objections of one major party or another concerning potential gain or loss of influence, not to mention a general fear of constitutional conventions by incumbent legislators. Regardless, from a voters perspective, any system that gives proportional meaning to their vote and also produces an adequate supply and spectrum of parties and candidates from which to choose would seem to be a vast improvement over two-party monopoly.

Today, the very idea of an electoral college tends to offend our hard-earned rights of suffrage and other democratic sensibilities. But looked at from another perspective, it is quite possible that a greatly expanded version of the college, were it given the power of nomination and ferreting out of people of merit for high office, might be a very useful institution. In other words, the benefits of republicanism could be better combined with the advantages of democracy. Local Electoral Colleges, on a small district basis, could lead to a rebirth of representative democracy, free from the overriding influence of major party apparatus and career politicians. New parties and independent candidates would have an opportunity to be heard from, and the views of the voters better measured by such an expanded college.

Who knows how many people of merit could be placed in public office were they approached by committees representing a bipartisan electoral college and asked to enter their name in nomination? As Alexander Hamilton observed, talent is not our problem: "There are strong minds in every walk of life that will rise superior to the disadvantages of station and will command the tribute due to their merit, not only from the classes to which they particularly belong, but from the society in general."[26] The question is purely one of barriers and access.

TRANSITIONS - IS WISDOM CUMULATIVE?

The facile rejoinder to a longer one-term approach is that somehow more is lost than gained. But in our current political scheme do we obtain the benefit of a valuable carry-over wisdom from reelected officials not available from new candidates? Or do career aspirations and self-interest often negate any such benefits? Would one-term legislators somehow be less discerning or prepared? Can we say that "old" legislators work as hard as "new" ones? And is it not possible that continually reelected legislators tend to become sloppy and lax in their approach to new issues and have less to offer? Do not career legislators develop fund-raising dependency, and hence a certain myopia on issues affecting the source of their campaign funds? Are our re-elected Presidents too preoccupied with "their place in history" for our own good? It is difficult to generalize regarding the answer to the question of experience, and there is no denying that many complex and agonizing issues face our legislators today. But the process of education regarding the issues, alternatives, and answers is the same regardless of length of term in office. What some may define as "experience" in our present system is often a perverted residue of incumbent political wisdom, accruing from longer term service, that is often bottled up, controlled, and effectively neutralized by special-interests. And what some may interpret as political "wisdom" today is simply pragmatism and an expedient notion of what can't be accomplished by those who wish to retain office.

Can legislators who have been continuously reelected, and survived a corrupt political environment, be fairly characterized as possessing a higher wisdom and independence? The truth may be exactly the opposite. What we don't appear to have today is true legislative independence and fearlessness - the indispensable virtues of any elected official. In contrast, single-term legislators could very well be effective and, more importantly, less dependent on outside influence. The reason is that one-term representatives would have, in large part, no future in politics. With the exception of those who may serve a term as senator or congressman and then be "drafted" to run for higher office this would be the case. The spectacle of those who attempt a lifetime career thru continuous reelection or jumping from office to office would soon incur the wrath of the voting public under a single term ethic. In addition, the motive and rational for serving a single term is likely to be different from those whose outlook is to carefully craft a long-term career via election or appointment.

But would we somehow be banning the growth of political experience and wisdom with a one-term solution as some critics might contend? A better question might be whether we will be attracting even more experience and wisdom by making public office respectable with single terms and true campaign finance reform. How many more professionals, from various fields, might we see stepping forward to place their name in nomination for public office once the circus is reformed?

Is political wisdom only acquired thru duration in office? It doesn't take many examples of present day legislators and their folly, participated in after decades of incumbency, to destroy this theory. The most "experienced" man to ever assume the presidency was James Buchanan who racked up 40 years of "service" in various elective and appointed positions to prepare him for the oval office.[27] But he was a dismal failure as president. On the other hand probably the least experienced man to become president was Abraham Lincoln. So much for the surefire test of experience.

Government is all about good management - a field in which private sector practitioners have most of the experience. But longevity and the accretion of undue power and influence has often led to the utter abuse of office by politicians who, by virtue of continuous reelection, acquired veto power over whole committees and legislative bodies. In this regard, we have only to consider the years of delays in the abolition of slavery, as well as the establishment of full civil rights for women and minorities, due solely to the efforts of a few "deadwood" senators whose political longevity gave them a stranglehold on powerful legislative committees. For decades the chairmanship of every major congressional and senate committee was in the hands of powerful southern congressmen and senators. This condition mirrored the old Soviet politburo where party members held sway for life and "reelection" was a virtual certainty. Because of this power they often ran unopposed. With this virtual "lock" on reelection, the irony is that these powerful officials did not answer to the voting public.

It is not unfair to say that longevity in office, as a working principle, has more often worked against the real interests of the nation than for it. Those inclined to oppose the idea of a single term might do well to attempt to recount the supposed benefits of having near lifelong representatives in office.

A smoother transition of power, and a more cooperative change of administration, is likely when one office-holder is replaced by another who has not been defeated in an election by their successor. The bitter remains of political battles often leave matters in administrative agencies and legislator's offices in a shambles. Election defeats hurt egos and result in lost effectiveness in transition. In a do-or-die electoral system the interests of the people suffer from all the unnecessary politics, campaigning, and disruption of duty involved.

In contrast, single-term office holders could well provide a smoother transition as they would have no axe to grind and no animosities toward their successors. It is hard to see where single-term transitions would engender the same problems as our present adversarial reelection process.

The essential question is how we must now re-arrange our electoral affairs to guarantee the body politic that the best men and women step forward to participate in government? How do the taxpayers, as opposed to the special-interests, get their money's worth of representation? And how shall we arrange our political affairs to obtain the smoothest of transitions between terms and changes of administration? Are short congressional terms and continual reelection, given the divisive and costly process involved, the way to insure effective continuity? I think not.

REPRESENTATION IN THE INFORMATION AGE —

"The use of knowledge as the principal commodity in Post-Industrial Society will tend to break down the rigidity of all hierarchal forms of management organization and replace these with more democratic participatory processes."[28]

J. McHale

Whether we favor it or not, electronic democracy is now a reality. Instant ratification of any proposal is now possible at a computerized ballot box. Yet few have considered how the changes wrought by the information age challenge the very rational and structure of our republic. Technology in the information age has the capacity to put the average voter "on line" with virtually the same information available to our representatives. The era of the priests and professions, built on secret information monopolies, is slowly dying. Today, the historical separation between voter, elector, and legislator has also been obliterated - we are now all of these simultaneously.

We live in a new age of instantaneous information flow and a reality of electronic voting. If our system needs overhaul we can "meet" in our satellite-connected living rooms and discuss the alternatives. Regardless, if we simply decide to elect new faces, who must labor under the same set of deficient political ground rules, we are not likely to change the results. Despite the promise of new technology, good government cannot grow out of a sewer of campaign finance corruption and rampant careerism.

The essential function of any legislator is to process information and translate our societal needs into public policy. Today the abilities of the representative and the average voter, to access and appraise policy studies, are nearly identical. And like most voters even legislators are not "experts" on every subject, or perhaps on any. As Will Rogers stated, "everybody is ignorant, only on different subjects." In this respect, the legislator's task is to simply digest the best and most reliable of material relating to the problem before a legislative decision is made.

This processing function, given the veritable explosion of "information" produced to influence policy, is certainly a full time job. But seeing the forest for the trees is often a function of distance and perspective more perfectly formed by the voters themselves. Regardless, our political traditions, as well as much of the original rational responsible for shaping our institutions, has been forever altered by the new media and computer technology. Technology has now elevated the abilities of the average voter and rendered obsolete the old style of passive republican politics. The new age of direct initiatives and the independent, and well-informed, one-term legislator is upon us.

THE VALUE OF POLITICAL EXPERIENCE —

> "The judgments of the 535 members of Congress, like anyone else's, can hardly be better than the information on which those judgments are made."[29]

> Joseph Califano

171

Despite the impact of technology, a single-term electoral system raises the question of the value of legislative experience per se. Incumbents, naturally, like to argue that judgment is somehow "improved" with multiple terms. But the fact is that the value of experience in office, per se, is greatly diminished by the ready availability of good information.

Legislators are simply macro-managers of our local, state, and national affairs. As a matter of necessity legislators hold hearings and evaluate studies of issues to arrive at appropriate legislative solutions. But ordinary good business management is essentially the same function. To maintain that single-term "novice" legislators, who may well have extensive private sector management experience, would somehow be at a disadvantage to, or less effective than, long-term incuments is to deny the reality of the information age and the validity of experience outside of political office. Naturally, you can expect to hear arguments of this type from career legislators fearful of a one-term solution.

Congress, like any decision making body, is dependent on good information. It is also heavily dependent on others for that information. PAC's and Lobbyists, federal agencies, and the Executive branch all deluge members of Congress with information on pending legislation. And whatever the source, there exists a tendency to control the very creation and dissemination of this "information" for political advantage. All three branches of government, distrustful of the motives of the other, are busy churning out their own sources of data and policy studies to advance their interests. In addition, legislators are bogged down with dubious data from lobbyists and political consultants.

Legislators estimate that 80-90% of Congress' information is generated by the Executive branch. In effect, Congress is spoonfed Executive branch propaganda. As Morris Udall stated: "Knowledge is power, and the decline in congressional power can be at least partially attributed to the inability of the legislative branch to develop information sources independent of the executive branch."[30] And what little information is not given to Congress by the White House will more than likely be provided by powerful lobbies and special-interests from their own enormous information creating resources.

In effect, legislators are now engulfed in a paperized "white plague" of politically structured "facts." But whether wisdom has exploded along with this increase in information is another matter. And information overload today is common to any representative, regardless of length of service. Senator James Buckley stated the obvious problem: "As for trying to do all the necessary reading, all that is required to develop in-depth personal understanding and knowledge, it can never be done. The amount of reading necessary to keep a senator minimally informed on matters of maximum importance is always double that which he can possibly accomplish in the time alloted."[31] The length of time in office, however, does not augment this essential process.

In a study of the effects of the information revolution on legislators, Stephen Frantzich noted in "Computers in Congress" how the arrival of the information society demands a radical "redefinition of personal competence" in legislative affairs. "The increasing codification and formalization of knowledge reduces the significance of personal experience."[32] Legislators today can no longer count on reaching old age with increasing responsibility, respect and remuneration. They are only as good as their information processing skills. The ability to bombast one's way thru multiple terms as a "successful" politician does not tell us anything about their skills as a legislator.

A mastery of information accessing and processing skills is essential for legislators today. Experience in political office, per se, no longer has as much relevance - you are only as good as your information. There are problems, and there are solutions. The new breed of legislators, with more familiarity and mastery of the information environment, will be more effective and less dogmatic than the old guard with their suppositions about reality such as Ronald Reagan's classic comment about trees causing pollution!

It may be unfortunate in one sense that age, experience, and incumbency count for less today then sheer analytical skills. And there is little question a need will always exist for great communicators and inspirational leaders as well as genuine wisdom and insight. But the possession of these qualities, or lack of, can in no way be linked with previous political experience.

AT-LARGE REPRESENTATIVES? —

Today we are all victims of our representative's personal conflicts of interest and failure to balance local and national concerns. The problem, as we have seen, is with the dual responsibilities of legislators. On the one hand, they must represent the concerns of their constituents and, on the other, be able to rise above merely parochial interests to meet the greater demands of the larger body politic.

One overlooked method to offset this basic conflict might be to simply increase the number of at-large representatives affiliated with a particular district. It is more apparent today that what we really need is a Congress without districts, a single body of meritorious at-large representatives. But while such a strategy upsets the theory of purely local representation it may well be an effective solution to the pork-barrel mentality and deficit prone behavior of Congress.

However, the Supreme Court has consistently mandated a strict mathematical equality in apportioning representation in the House of Representatives, despite the lack of such authority in the constitution. The principle of "one person-one vote" was outlined in the 1962 case of Baker v. Carr.[33] The court declared that each member of a legislative body should represent an equal number of persons. Obviously, the ideal of a free and properly functioning election process is that representatives will reflect the will of the people. But our problem is that Congress contains "535 peoples" involved in a war over federal dollars.

More recent court decisions, from the 9th Circuit Court of Appeals, have held that At-large representation can be challenged by minorities who may consider the color of a representative to be more important than the bent of their minds. Ironically, with this racist logic we will forever be attempting to elect people on the very basis of color and ethnicity rather than merit and proceeding to eliminate all racial considerations. And with attention diverted to achieving perfect "rainbow" representation, rather than pure considerations of merit, the likelihood of future legislative stalemates is increased.

Apparently, the courts believe a "rainbow coalition" thru at-large representation is somehow unachievable. But that may well be precisely what we need. The success of both Jesse Jackson as a presidential candidate, and other victorious black and brown politicians across the nation, readily dispels the theory of "minority" exclusion. Even our verbiage no longer describes reality due to the fact that, in many urban locations today, whites are now a minority.

But the essential problem is not the color of one's skin but that of voter participation and not removing the at-large format from our political arsenal. If the courts continue to mandate our political separation into "wards" and tight ethnic districts our problems will only multiply.

The Court has also deemed that gerrymanders, multi-member districts, at-large constituencies, and other super-majority requirements may fail to meet the one person-one vote test. And where an obvious historical pattern of racial discrimination exists such may be the case. But multi-member districts and at-large representation are not, per se, invalidated. Certainly the senate itself is not built on proportional representation and was specifically excluded from this court requirement because of the clear intent of the framers of the constitution. But if we are ever to escape the stranglehold of 535 districts acting in "their own best interests" to the detriment of the nation we should reconsider the idea of at-large representation.

For instance, if voters in a particular state voted for their proportional number of unaffiliated representatives or, indeed, if the entire congress were elected at-large, the problems of district rapacity might be obviated, or at least greatly reduced. Under such a plan representatives of merit and integrity could emerge and supplant party careerists interested in dominating district politics.

As a nation, our problem is that district representatives are bound to be prisoners of local demands. But single-term, at-large, representatives would be less apt to be beholden to specific localities, industries, or interest groups based in a particular community. The problem of allegiance and loyalty is thus raised to a higher factor and a larger constituency. In this way, more at-large representation would help to mitigate the primal and counterproductive territoriality of congress.

The inability of Congress to attack the major problems of our day is largely due to the nature of each representative's loyalties to localized constituencies and the magnified effect of special-interests under a reelection system gone wrong. A case could be made for expanding the House of Representatives by one at-large legislator for each district representative. Of course, this approach also undermines the very rationale and purpose of the senate.

In effect, at-large representation raises the horizons of the legislator. The senate aside, more such representation is now necessary and feasible due to the increased size and sheer incoherence of many congressional "districts." In fact, most representatives are, in one sense, at-large anyway given the very size of their districts. A legislator who represents a half million people cannot be said to be on intimate terms with his constituents. Regardless, the size of one's constituency should be manageable and not a result of constant gerrymandering by the incumbents themselves.

The task of getting better government, at any level, will necessitate achieving a better balance between at-large and local representatives. When one considers that each state has its own government to handle internal problems, the necessity of electing purely district representatives to the federal level of problem solving leaves one wondering about the wisdom of such fragmented representation. If states had only at-large representatives to the federal level, these relatively unattached "electors" might bring a fairer, and less affiliated perspective to the problems of their district as well as the nation. The macro perspective, the management of the nation as a whole, would benefit while micro-loyalties and pork-barrel schemes would justifiably suffer.

With district representatives, Congress tends not to solve but to exacerbate problems of national scope. If Congress were doubled in size by the addition of one at-large representative, elected on a state-wide basis, we would have a better balanced body of representatives able to solve our national problems. Perhaps like the electors originally envisioned by the framers, at-Large delegates could become stay-at-home legislators free from the capitol political atmosphere. They can vote from the nearest computer terminal. And, best of all, these extra representatives would not need duplicate staffs, office space, pensions and the endless perquisites that only bleed the taxpayer.

With such a plan we might have a chance to break up our national legislative gridlock. Solutions to our major problems of national scope; the deficit, streamlining of the federal bureaucracy, pollution, trade relations, etc., would most certainly accrue to the benefit of all states of the union. And local concerns would still be adequately voiced, but not over represented to the extent that interminable conflict and deadlock is the only result. The Senate's function, under such an arrangement, becomes somewhat questionable, but nonetheless necessary. The Senate is simply an at-large body of state representatives. But it serves as a repository of senior statesmen and distinguished citizens able to perform the "advise and consent" functions.

In another sense we are living a political fiction. Our state borders are illusory. The lines on the map that separate the lower forty-eight states are imaginary. Boundaries are nonexistent or fluid at best. And what we have are representatives dedicated to maintaining political and geographical fictions. In addition, our "districts" and state lines are largely unrelated to real bioregions or coherent economic zones.

Thus we are politically schizophrenic by design. What are we? A nation, or a collection of states? If we are not truly one nation then perhaps we would be better off as fifty nations. How can we attempt to solve our national problems with district-tied state representatives?

Reality dictates that we transcend and eliminate borders that separate us from solutions to our common problems. Here, the type and scope of representation is crucial. If regional loyalties crush the at-large instincts of our representatives, we are doomed. Our devastating world-wide environmental problems will necessitate more ad-hoc global forums with competitive nations compelled to cooperate for our common survival. The at-large macro viewpoint is a political necessity. Unless we are successful in controlling parochial factionalism and special-interest cartels we will only produce more bombast and carbon dioxide ensuring the demise of all nations and even our world. On the positive side, such at-large, ad-hoc, forums may well be the birthsites of a new age of world-wide peace and prosperity.

In other words, the "global village" is becoming a reality. And much like the melting of European nations into a "common market" we need to melt our states into a more workable commons. The maintenance of national political arrangements from an age when the original colonies were more like soverign nations into an era where time and distance no longer have meaning is, as we have seen, simply self-defeating. The truth is that our states today are not all that separate, or united.

BICAMERAL NONSENSE? —

Was the senate created as a representational afterthought, or is it an indispensable body of reason above the rabble? And what is the rational for a senate, or "higher" House, unless one believes that a body of fewer members, with longer terms of office, are liable to be more productive and responsible than a body of many members with shorter terms? The rational of a senate is thus the rational of a one-term solution.

The existence of a senate may well have been deemed necessary by a majority of the framers to properly represent the established money, wealth, and power of their day. The polite term was that it was to serve as a "check and balance" against an assembly of those less rich and well-dressed farmers and small merchants. However, in our egalitarian age, characterized by the presence of a broad middle class in a more "democratic" society, such rationale is simply outdated. Over two centuries later, the class distinctions that may once have existed between members of Congress and the Senate are less apparent if not altogether nonexistent.

The original rational for a bicameral arrangement may well have reflected a need not only for "checks and balances" but also for the less evident and unstated reason to maintain prevailing social class distinctions and privileges. The very existence of a senate with ratification power over a popular assembly, as opposed to a unicameral national legislature, probably owes more to the class consciousness and social divisions present in the late eighteenth century than we care to acknowledge today. The stated rational was to equalize the representation and power of the large and small states. But if we were to hold another Constitutional Convention today, would there still be a rational for a second body, an elite? Would we devise similar institutions or simply settle on a district, or an at-large, format?

While the chances for converting to a national unicameral legislature are slim that is not to say we cannot question the current relevance and efficacy of a dual body government. There will always be checks and balances between the Judicial, the Executive, and the Legislative branches of government. But does it help, in this day and age, to confuse the issues by having two separate national legislative bodies? Indeed, one can argue that it may now be a liability.

That is not to say that a unicameral "direct democracy" is necessarily a good idea or more capable of producing better government than a properly functioning republic. The point is simply that extra layers of government in our modern bicameral "republic" may be dysfunctional and produce more checks than balance.

Today, the real effect of the senate is to give smaller states a larger representation and power than is justified by their population. This was an essential compromise to forge a union of states with unequal populations and resources. From another perspective, however, the longer terms of the senate also seem to have empowered members of the "higher" house to be more visible, as well as more productive and responsible to a national constituency. Thus the senate has performed a valuable congressional oversight function at times. However, with longer single congressional terms the need for such senatorial oversight may not even arise.

It is certainly possible we might do things differently at a Constitutional Convention today given that some of the original rationale for the creation and shaping of our institutions is no longer the same, or might be viewed as repugnant in this century. A new convention today would have trouble proceeding towards a strict bicameral republic, as opposed to a more egalitarian unicameral democracy, especially in our new age of instantaneous vote transmission.

CHAPTER VI

— JUSTICE FOR SALE —

POLITICS IN THE COURTROOM —

> "The people with money to spend who are affected by court decisions have reached the conclusion that its a lot cheaper to buy a judge than a governor or an entire legislature and he can probably do a lot more for you."[1]
>
> Leslie Jacobs, Ohio Bar Assoc.

* * *

> "What's at stake here is the actual integrity of the judiciary in almost all the states of the union."[2]
>
> Roy Schotland

With so much media attention focused on national political campaigns, the fact that our judiciary system is slowly being devoured by the same cancer of campaign finance corruption is escaping the attention of the public. A very distubing trend is undermining our courts - the election of judges and the resultant politicization of our judicial system. This new trend would surely cause the founding fathers to turn over in their graves.

Unbeknownst to many voters, there are now 38 states of the union that elect judges at the trial, appellate or state Supreme Court level.[3] Unfortunately, the same money-media demands and insidious campaign finance problems are corrupting our judiciary as well as our political offices.

In effect, judges today are presiding over cases in which one or both parties in court may have contributed to the Judge's election or reelection campaign. Tragically, the one arena that we thought might have remained above partisan politics is now being devoured by it. Judges now solicit money for reelection campaign expenses like ordinary politicians. As a result, our justice system now has the appearance of being for sale.

The judicial campaign finance process is ever so subtle and unspoken but nevertheless pernicious. Conflict-of-interest is becoming pervasive in our courtrooms. But this fact is often little known to anyone other than the participants in judicial campaign giving. It is truly unfortunate that we have so many jurisdictions operating today under a politicized system in which "justice" may be for sale. But with an elective system for judges, similar to legislators, the same demands for campaign and media expenses prevail. And who is going to contribute to pay those expenses? The answer is anyone with an interest in pending or future litigation - lawyers, litigants, and defendants with a lot to lose. And who is going to win? Incumbent judges hold all the cards.

Common Cause has outlined the current dilemma with elected judges and the systemic conflict of interest arising from their reelection demands. They point out that, in Illinois and other states, candidates for judicial office may even convert election campaign contributions to personal funds after the election. In other words, even the loser can profit by promising influence during his or her campaign. In addition, in some states (Texas) there is no time limit on campaigning so that fundraising can go on continuously - corruption never ends.[4]

By subjecting judges to reelection rather than longer single terms, we are simply trashing our system of justice and asking for the worst of abuses. Here, again, the one-term solution is an appropriate remedy for a justice system where judges must now sacrifice their impartiality and independence to bend with the political winds.

In effect, we could hardly design a more advantageous situation for judicial bribery than what already exists in these states. If one has a case before a judge whose reelection campaign you did not contribute to, perhaps in favor of his opponent, you may have cause to worry. You may also need to inform your client! The essential question is why attorneys would even consider contributing to other than an incumbent if they have pending business before the court? Gerald Richman, a former President of the Florida Bar stated: "I had a case before a judge and her campaign committee solicited an endorsement and money while there was a non-jury case before her... I endorsed the judge but wouldn't give a monetary contribution while the case was pending. The day before the case went to court I got a call thanking me for the endorsement but saying 'we noted that there was no check.'"[5] Judicial incumbency, under the present system, is a threat to justice where money for reelection is a necessity. This is the sad reality of reelection justice today.

To make matters worse, unlike most PAC donations, campaign contributors to judicial campaigns may hide their affiliation with particular groups who may have concerns pending in important court cases. Contributors are not usually required to identify themselves by occupation. Thus concentrated donations from a particular profession or interest group, with judicial business pending, cannot be easily detected. Gerald Stern, of the New York State Commission on Judicial conduct stated: "Ninety percent of the contributions in New York come from lawyers... Obviously, that presents some ethical problems."[6] Indeed.

When we consider the magnitude of decisions pending in the commercial arena (such as the Texaco-Pennzoil case in which preliminary judgements reached 10 Billion in damages!) we get some idea of the money involved in legal matters upon which a single elected judge may have sway.

Our courts are on the verge today of becoming tiny banana republics, with black-robed dictators soaking up funds from the legal community while compromising their own integrity and the public trust. Conflict of interest will remain pervasive under elective systems that necessitate money for expensive media campaigns. And real awareness of complicated legal issues will suffer when reduced to 15 and 30-second campaign "spots" for public consumption.

The result of such election campaigns on our judiciary is obvious. Leslie Jacobs, of the Ohio Bar Association, pbserved: "Once elected... you're incapable of serving."[7] In other words, the conflicts of interest created by acceptance of donations from lawyers, as well as defendant's and plaintiff's groups, make it ethically impossible for a judge to hear many cases. However, we don't see judges disqualifying themselves from hearing such cases in states with judicial elections. And yet we know that a higher standard of legal practice demands such a course of behavior.

> "It's unseemly to think of wearing the robes of the
> highest court, from which there is no appeal in
> virtually all cases, and taking the robes off at night
> to go to special-interest groups' meetings."[8]

Judge Bruce Kauffmann

The politicalization of our courts is not the solution to achieving an independent judiciary. It is an impediment that must be removed and replaced with a better system - a one-term merit appointment solution.

MERIT SELECTION FOR JUDGES —

Eliminating the process of both election, and reelection, from our judiciary would greatly restore the possibility of impartiality in our court system. Only merit appointments by qualified and widely diversified civic and professional groups, without interests in pending legal matters, are likely to insure that judges remain free from the corruption of elective politics.

And as long as recall is a viable option, in the case of unsatisfactory or derelict appointments, the merit system of judicial selection is the best choice for our courts. Elections only bring the cult of personality, and the corruption of campaign financing into our courtrooms and force judges to become politicians. For judges, as well as legislators, it is the election process itself, and especially reelection, that is the basic problem and not the solution.

As Alexander hamilton observed: "Next to permanancy in office, nothing can contribute more to the independence of the judges than a fixed provision for their support... In the general course of human nature, a power over a man's subsistence amounts to a power over his will."9 Unfortunately, the necessity of reelection and fundraising gives special-interests just such a power over a judge's professional "subsistence" and will.

The Supreme Court, and court of last resort, is a very hallowed institution in our political system. The high court is our Mt. Olympus, our Oracle of Delphi and national seat of wisdom and truth beyond approach. The framers understood the high court should be above reproach and beyond influence. For this reason the life appointment was considered appropriate for a Supreme Court Justice but no other elective or appointive office in the land.

However, a "life" term can be a very long appointment - perhaps too long. A judge appointed in his forties can easily spend 40 years or more on the high court. Is this desirable? One president, with five appointments in his term, can change the nature of the court for literally half a century! Is this a systemic flaw? This is yet another area where we need to rethink our approach and seriously consider structural changes in our system of judicial appointments.

Why appointments for life? Why not one long term like a Federal Reserve Governor, say 14 years. Why should one president be able to "pack" the court for decades beyond his own term and time? I am not necessarily implying that we should emulate the early nineteenth century provision of the state of New York prohibiting a man from sitting as a judge after the age of sixty, but merely that a reasonable length of term would keep the court contemporary.

Such a system of 14-year appointments for Supreme Court justices would then open the highest judicial office to a few more able and qualified legal scholars during their, and our, lifetimes. The ability of a president to appoint five persons to the bench who may conceivably serve for a half-century must be said to be well beyond the "intent" of the framers. This is carrying the idea of permanence, considered necessary to remain immune to political influence, to an unneccessary and perhaps deleterious extreme. One president, a 51% plurality dictator, can see to it that a five judge "majority" legal fascism prevails for decades.

The clear intent of the writers of the constitution was that all judges appointed by the United States would hold their office "during good behavior." In effect, the appointment was for life, but the impeachment remedy was always at hand for the most errant of appointees. But life-spans were not what they are today. Thus a "life-term" has taken on new meaning.

As for the lower courts, the framers of the constitution did not contemplate that we would ever have a judicial system where judges are subject to reelection and thus open to the same corrupting influences that plague our legislators. Such a state of affairs was simply out of the question. Here again we see the mere passage of time does not necessarily bring "progress" or improvements in our political systems. We need to reexamine the judiciary and return to merit appointments by diverse bipartisan bodies. Otherwise our courts, and justice itself, will remain under a cloud of suspicion.

CHAPTER VII

— THE MEDIA AND POLITICS —

TELEVISION AND POLITICS —

"If you're not on television, you don't exist."[1]

A Gubernatorial candidate

* * *

"There's only two things in politics now - money
and media. The day of the grass roots organization
is a a thing of the past. It's all money and media."[2]

Phillip Stern

* * *

"The idea that you can merchandise candidates for
high office like breakfast cereal... is the ultimate
indignity to the democratic process."[3]

Adlai Stevenson

There is no question our political system has been
impacted heavily, first by radio, and now by television. The
power and influence of these modern media were unseen by
our founders who lived at a time when representatives had
to travel by horseback or carriage for hours and days to get
from their home districts to the statehouse or capital. There
was time for reflection on important issues. The pace of
deliberation and decision was altogether different for our
eighteenth-century representatives.

In today's political climate, however, there now exists a very potent and dangerous symbiosis of money, media, power, and politics. Direct and immediate "communication" with the voters via television has supplanted the townhall representative system that served the original thirteen colonies so well. Despite our media power most voters relationships with their representatives today are either nonexistent or fleeting in the extreme.

However immediate our communication, it is still "managed" and controlled by political organizations and major networks that filter and define what is "news." Local events often go unreported while national and international mega-events soak up precious media time. Television has thrust us into the world without grounding us in our own communities. Our growing numbers of urbanites, and suburbanites, are now more politically rootless than ever before.

Despite the daily deluge of "news" voters seem to know very little about political affairs and their representative's votes. Ironically, knowledge of local affairs is worst of all - City Hall is nearly invisible. Television today fills us with macro-news, events happening half-a-world away, but we know very little about the micro-events shaping our immediate world. Too many important matters at City Hall and the State House are left uncovered and almost completely unknown to the local populace. Voters know more about disasters in the far corners of the earth than about disastrous representation in their own neighborhoods.

Politics has become a series of media events - structured encounters with a camera and press releases designed to impress the voters. The only time our media seems to work well is when a selection of candidates is presented in a non-structured debate forum - one in which the real personalities and responses can emerge unfettered by slick scripted positions. Unfortunately, we have no laws to date that give the people, and not the candidates, the power to set the rules for such debate.

In a modern gridlocked world the likelihood of many voters even getting to a central town hall meeting is now almost out of the question. Thus, televised political debates take on huge significance in our time. But since the famous five o'clock shadow problem did in Richard Nixon during his debate with the young and handsome John F. Kennedy, the unspoken rule is not to debate your opponent and give them additional exposure. Only in the primaries, among candidates of the same party, do we continue to see any meaningful debates for public consumption.

A rational political system will have an institutionalized and mandatory system of debates between presidential and gubernatorial candidates, at a very minimum. Otherwise, we are indirectly supporting the incumbent and stunting our political growth. For candidates and incumbents to be able to hide from their opponents, and the voters, simply cannot be an option.

Despite television's presence, real debate has not emerged as an on-going process in our elections. Indeed, as a rule, the majority of incumbents refuse to debate challengers or, at the very least, cripple any such encounters with altogether asinine restrictions. Thus the incumbent, in effect, has the power to deny media access to challengers. But no candidate or incumbent should have this choice - public debate must be mandatory.

In the 1988 election campaign, the League of Women Voters actually refused to sponsor the follow-up presidential debate due to silly groundrules from the candidates turning any potential for real debate into prepared and scripted rhetoric to be spoonfed to the public. In view of the fact that aspiring candidates will eventually work for the taxpayers there is simply no way that they should be able to refuse debate, or control its groundrules, in a rational republic so dependent on media communication. This is one area where voters have clearly lost control over their legislators and why incumbents have stolen the show.

On the other hand, television has given us the potential to eliminate the old party-centered campaign and concentrate on independent and qualified individuals. But instead, due to the lack of any alternative political organizations with the buying power of the major parties, it seems only to prop up the two party affair. Inertia alone explains the system.

Prior to radio and television, voters received most of their information about issues and candidates thru the auspices and filters of party-controlled newspapers. But the older class-based divisions of labor and management, that long formed the philosophical basis of the major parties, have been greatly weakened by the growth of the middle-class and the extension of the franchise to women and minorites. In addition, the impact of television, radio, and direct-mail has all but buried the party system. About all that remains for a party organization to do is to raise money and get out the vote on election day. Otherwise, they play almost no role in the selection, as opposed to the coronation, of the candidate. The entire affair is in the hands of the political and media consultants.

It is obvious the relationship between voters and their representative has changed significantly over the course of our republic. A legislator's campaign consultants now view their constituency in terms of "blocs" and segmented market shares based around simple and single issues. Communication with the voters via direct mail is fine-tuned to the characteristics of the constituent in the particular zip code. Sophisticated date-processing technology now targets each "geodemographic" block and matches voter preferences with mail-order literature. Manipulation is by cluster group and issues that appeal to the particular class of voters - zip code politics has arrived.

In other words, we are manipulated by our representatives on a vast scale. And they use taxpayer's money to do so.

Personalities now prevail in media-centered politics. At the same time issues and party platforms have been reduced in importance, if for no other reason than such specifics provide ammunition for negative attacks by your opponent. Telegenic candidates, and fifteen-second TV spots, are the rule of the day. Winston Churchill wouldn't stand a chance on television.

> "The truth is that anyone who knows what he is doing can say what he is doing, and anyone who knows what he thinks can say what he thinks. Those who cannot speak for themselves are, with very rare exceptions, not very sure of what they are doing and of what they mean. The sooner they are found out the better."[4]

Walter Lippman

Perhaps a major reason behind voter apathy today is that the modern political arena is plagued with ghost-written and teleprompted candidates whose own inabilities to declare their positions are masked by structured media events and the efforts of legions of speechwriters and consultants. Eloquence, debate, and open public discourse, displaying the true measure of a candidate, is being sytematically denied the voters. Spontaneity is dead and avoided in the heat of the campaign. But open and unscripted debate must be a requirement for all candidates and incumbents or the electorate will not become well-informed and feel comfortable with their choices.

In a television environment increasingly saturated with political cartoons, it is easy to understand why voter turnouts, with the exception of presidential contests, have hit all-time lows in recent years. Many local and national candidates are now elected with only a 20-25% turnout of eligible voters. Voters have been turned off by the media circus we call politics, and media neglect of local matters only compounds our problems.

But not all is bleak. Television has also made possible the rise of the insurgent "maverick" candidate with only nominal affiliation with a major party to achieve the highest office in the land. The campaign of Jimmy Carter is a good example of this phenomenoa. The fact that a popular maverick candidate can now emerge and outmanuever the major parties and special-interests is, I believe, a healthy phenomenoa.

191

However, the potential for telegenic politicians, with their hands on the latest polls, to message their way into office can also be a mixed blessing. A "great communicator" is not necessarily going to be a good legislator. But increased access to high office by visible and popular candidates, free of traditional party ties and special-interest obligations, is a plus for an electorate tired of the old ways and desirous of fundamental change.

WHO OWNS OUR AIRWAVES? —

> "Television has now become the accepted medium for selling political candidates... although Congress passed a law that requires stations to sell time to political candidates at a discount, in practice it frequently works out the opposite way... because the peak period for reaching voters is of limited duration candidates often find themselves paying premium rates to bump commercial advertisers from the choicest evening spot-announcement times. The net result is that political candidates are indebting themselves to special-interest contributions in large part to add to local broadcasters' already stupendous profits. The whole spectacle is obscene."[5]
>
> Phillip Stern

The people of the United States are the ultimate owners of our airwaves and broadcast licenses. It may now be time to up the rent and require lessees to set aside adequate amounts of time for political spots within, say, ninety days of federal elections. With more public control over allocation of media time to candidates, voters can short-circuit special-interest financing and control of our election process.

One approach to broadening media access was proposed by Senator William Fulbright during FCC hearings on media access in 1970. He suggested legislating "public service time" thru amendments to the 1934 Communications Act. His resolution read: "Broadcast licensees shall provide a reasonable

amount of public service time to authorized representatives...
to present the views of the Senate and the House of
Representatives on issues of public importance. The public
service time required to be provided... shall be made available
to each such authorized representative at least, but not limited
to, four times during each calendar year."[6]

The essence of Fulbright's proposal was to guarantee
the right of the people to hear diverse and opposing views
regardless of party or regional affiliation. However, even this
proposal was incumbent-based and limited to members of the
House and Senate. And without clear provisions for public
access the media can pick and choose their coverage of
important national debates. As private profit-making
enterprises, the networks will likely opt to air profitable game
shows rather than donate any "public service time" on all but
the most sensational of occasions. This is a modern day tragedy
and one of the prime reasons we have so little public
participation in politics. Out-of-sight, out-of mind, and out-
of-office is the dilemma of our political opposition today.

With a president's power to request prime-time television
coverage, the problem of "fairness" and equal access to media
has become an important problem. But fairness, as presently
defined, is still limited to traditional parties and elected officials.
The limits of the "fairness doctrine" itself need to be examined.

In other democracies around the world there is generally
more government control of media and provision for public
debate. In the United States, however, we have almost a virtual
blackout of debate in our political institutions. With the very
important exception of the Corporation for Public
Broadcasting, airing publicly sponsored radio and television,
we are left only with paid television commercials at election
time.

In Sweden, where the government and the people own
all the broadcast media there is no problem of access or fairness
to minority or unpopular viewpoints. And a thirst for consensus
fuels political debate. Further, private newspapers still serve
the function of standard bearers for traditional factions and

parties. Many other democracies have come to the conclusion that the medium of television is too influential, and politics too important, to rely totally on the good judgment of private interests to display their democracy in action.

In Mexico, where a new generation of politicians have begun to put an end to corrupt political practices, the 1987 revisions to the Federal Electoral Code mandated free air time on all radio and television stations for each party, regardless of size. In the latest election about 51 hours per party were allocated.[7] The predictable result was debate was enlivened and participation blossomed despite lingering doubts about election fraud. We must contrast this type of full spectrum access and debate to the United States and our major networks coverage of the recent presidential campaigns, where only two political parties have a media existence. In many respects, our media politics are an embarrassment to a "free country." Do we dare call ourselves a free country where everything has a price, including "free speech."

Can voters reform the impact of television on politics? Will we be able to reclaim a portion of our "licensed" airwaves for important public debate and thereby cut the costs and corruption of campaigns? Public affairs should not be structured to benefit, and be controlled by, the private media interests and "lessees" of our airwaves. The time has come to re-examine the rights of the body politic to media access, and to recapture a portion of network airtime in order to diminish the role of special-interests in paying the politician's bill for exhorbitant media expenses. We are already paying for our air time in more ways than one.

The last thing we want is total government control of our radio and television stations. However, we also cannot allow special-interests to own the airwaves as well as the candidates who gain access to the media. New reform must achieve a middle-ground thru some combination of greater public financing of our political campaigns and a larger share of "private" media time reserved for legitimate public affairs.

TELEPOLITICIANS —

Unfortunately, we have no magic indicators to judge the people that flash across our television screens in search of political office. Still many are never seen. It is a fact that most of our congressional representatives are literally invisible thru election after election. We may notice a bumper sticker, a billboard, or a television advertisement but we rarely get a good glimpse of the people who control the purse strings of our nation. This is particularly true in our large urban areas where legislators may represent thousands of voters who cannot even remember their representative's name - incumbents like it this way.

As a result, the vast majority of voters today have a relationship only with a "telegenic" figure who appears on television with scripted positions derived from opinion polls. Sadly, it is only the special-interest groups that maintain an on-going relationship with the officeholder throughout the term. Constituents have become a remote lumpen mass to be interacted with only at reelection time. In a final insult to the ideal of "representation" the voters own scant opinions about complicated issues are polled and then spoon-fed back to them in the form of reassuring slogans designed to keep the incumbent in power.

In effect, this manipulative power has tended to jaundice the eye of the office holder toward their constituency. The urban nature of our society, and the sheer impersonality of large political districts, has given us the age of the invisible congressional representative. This state of affairs certainly falls short of the ideal republic. And after a life-time of watching Greek city-states in action, Plato suggested that the ideal size of a manageable republic, or coherent community, should not exceed 5,000 persons.[8] Beyond that the evils of impersonality, irresponsibility, and apathy would begin to appear. Today, with legislative districts containing hundreds of thousands of people, we are far from Plato's ideal political community.

Add to this witch's media brew the fact that our political process is now firmly in the hands of the manipulators, the media consultants, the pollsters, the look-good, feel-good, jockeys of american opinion who "package" the candidates for public consumption. The "selling of the president" and other candidates is now a prime concern of legions of political operatives who carefully sculpt our "image" of the politician.

Candidates have become actors and, logically, actors have become politicians. The political actor-candidate attacks our real life problems with a "script" written for the voters. Thus spontaneity, honesty, and gut-level directness have all but disappeared from our stage-managed political encounters. Voters are now treated like voyeurs who do not participate in the civic drama written by media professionals. For example, former Reagan Chief of Staff, Don Regan revealed the behind the scenes reality of the Reagan administration: "He (Reagan) regarded his daily schedules as being something like a shooting script in which characters came and went, scenes were rehearsed and acted out, and the plot was advanced one day at a time."[9]

But no matter how omnipresent our media, our new "global village" environment and fully media-ized nuclear households do not replicate the veritable townhall meeting place. The townhall of yesterday was a forum of encounter for the representative and voters. But we cannot truly compare the politics of the late eighteenth century with those of today. Certainly, a republican and representative style of government was in full flower in an era where communication was limited to horse-carried mail. Time and distance still had meaning and impact. But the immediacy and tempo of events today have given us an environment in which candidates are made and broken in a split-second by the fret of their brow or a slip of the tongue.

And in a world in which so many know so little about their government and constitution, and where polls have often shown that a majority of voters did not even recognize, or approve of, most of the provisions of our Bill of Rights, we must conclude that our schools, and the medium of television, have failed to serve their purpose. Ignorance and apathy in political affairs can be traced to media obsession with the lurid and spectacular. The decline of literacy puts an even greater burden on the medium of television to educate voters, expose politicians, and illuminate the entire spectrum of politics.

The problem of lopsided media availability to the party in power, or candidate in office, creates a dangerous political imbalance and serves to exclude the opposition and perpetuate incumbency. I believe these imbalances in our political system need adjustment thru new media access rules and a one-term solution.

CHAPTER VIII

— CONCLUSIONS AND RECOMMENDATIONS —

A FUTURE PREAMBLE —

> "We, the people, in order to form a *still* more perfect
> union, and correct abuses in our political system,
> hereby declare our intent to convene a
> Constitutional Convention for the consideration
> of amendments regarding term of office of
> Congressmen, Senators, Judges, and the President
> of the United States...

Will we soon see a Second Constitutional Convention?
I think so. Reform is in the air, and the next time american
voters convene, en masse, debate will not likely be limited to
insignificant issues. Instead, important structural changes in
our system of representation will be considered. And one very
important option will be a one-term solution.

As political and economic frustration mounts amongst
the electorate our awareness and discussion of options will
increase. This future-consciousness will propel us into a new
and healthy re-examination of our political institutions. We
will become more rebellious and akin to our eighteenth century
counterparts. We are on the verge of significant political change.

Alvin Toffler, a modern futurist, pointed out two
problems with modern electorates: first; a lack of future-
consciousness, and second; a lack of participation.[1] These two
factors alone keep voters from launching true reform and their
representatives from proper planning and preventing our

lurching from crisis to crisis. Our political system is short-sighted and "future-blind." This blindness is fed by the dubious necessity and immediacy of reelection campaigns. We are periodically drowned in platitudes, followed by periods of inaction and delay, until the next election circus. Our promised future never arrives.

But the nature of government is slowly changing today. And just where real power resides in an unfettered media democracy is still unclear. However, out of necessity, the public must regain control of the political process to protect themselves, and future generations, from their elected representatives.

While everyone laments the reality of politics today, few alternatives for changing the nature of the way we do business in our centers of political power seem to emerge. A one-term solution is one approach to the problem. But it could be a very important beginning in the transformation of political life and participation in government.

Under such a new civic regime, those whose dominate motives are the aquisition of wealth and power, and who remain relatively uninterested in the process and business of government, will seek their fortunes in the private sector. And more qualified people, who see government as service and civic duty, and have the character and secure professional or financial base from which to enter and leave politics gracefully, will come forward to be nominated and elected.

The tragedy of maintaining our system as it is today, is that we are continuing to breed a "corrosive cynicism" about politics in general and, especially, about participation in our local, state, or national governments. This cancer of indifference, reflected in small voting turnouts today, is stark evidence of a widespread disallusionment.

The time has come to rethink how we turn over our political duties and destinies to individuals whom we expect to remain pure as the driven snow while they attempt to survive in a corrupt system. Human nature being what it is, we ask for more than most of our representatives can supply. Our flaws are not merely human but structural.

For this reason the people, as a whole, must periodically take the helm and re-direct the entire ship of state. At the same time, we must wake to our reality. And we must judge our representatives and their accomplishments on the basis of the condition of our cities, towns, neighborhoods, and the world around us, as well as the sheer magnitude of unmet obligations. Effective legislators must enable us to account for our sins of the past and secure provisions for the future.

Political neglect and the inability of our political representatives to face difficult issues has finally caught up with us. In this regard, Hazel Henderson outlined the political challenge of the future stemming from the neglected underside of our culture: "While the commercial media have projected images of split-level suburban life styles conducive to satisfying the needs for a mass-consumption economy, citizen movements, whether for peace, consumer and environmental protection, or social equality, have focused on the unpublicized, the unresearched, and often suppressed information that constitutes the other side of the coin of industrial and technological development. The reason this information is suppressed is that it deals with the unintended side effects, the second-order consequences of the action of our political and economic institutions."[2]

The time has come for us to attend to the second-order consequences of our modern industrial democracy. These same second-order problems are generated and exacerbated, in large part, by the very nature of our present corrupt political system. And if we simply extrapolate our recent political past into the future we have cause to worry. C.P. Snow observed that "a sense of the future is behind all good politics. Unless we have it, we can give nothing - either wise or decent to the world."[3] In other words, good politicians don't borrow from the future.

Structural reform of the election process, along with a lengthening of basic terms of office, increased media access, and increased public campaign funding will effectively change our world. After such reforms, we may then have a political environment in which the great problems of our day can be faced courageously and, with foresight, perhaps solved to the lasting benefit of future generations.

Many in the United States today are losing faith in the institution of Congress and our elected representatives. Recent polls reflect the loss of confidence Americans have in their goverment in general. This despair is compounded by the obscene spectacle of the reelection syndrome and special-interests sway over our representatives. Without reelection reform political spirit is likely to continue to whither.

As a nation, our constitutional checks clearly do not balance anymore. Our political institutions, no longer energized by the civic spirit of the late eighteenth-century, are dead or barely responsive. The framers compromise on terms of office, reelection, and other political remedies, perhaps appearing to be effective in their own time, is no longer a match for the fundamental social, economic, and technological changes of the twenty-first century.

The one-term solution is one avenue for change that holds the promise of greatly enlivening our political process and breaking the stranglehold of incumbents and traditional parties. Ultimately, without true political reform, the vested interests that so effectively divert attention to rights, without mention of our responsibilities, will wreak havoc on the nation and the earth.

Recommmendations for further political action:
1. One-term six-year presidency.
2. One-term four-year congressional term.
3. One-term six-year senate terms.
4. Prohibition on holding more than four elective offices in a lifetime.
5. Nomination of presidential, and vice-presidential candidates, by nationwide primary.
6. Nomination of Attorneys General by bipartisan groups.

7. Federal financing of Congressional and Senate campaigns. State financing of Gubernatorial and local campaigns.
8. Presidential primaries no more than six months from date of general election (in absence of nationwide primary).
9. Campaign fund-raising prohibitions more than one year from date of election, with exception of new parties.
10. Elimination of judicial elections - nomination only thru bipartisan citizen and professional groups.
11. Elimination of judicial "life" appointments.
12. Bipartisan "Electoral College" style nominating bodies to augment, or eliminate, self-nomination for elective office.
13. Elimination of 5% previous vote requirement and 20-state requirement for "matching funds" for new candidates and parties.
14. Elimination of tenure in public employment.
15. Require television media time "givebacks" for political debate between local, state, and national candidates.
16. Candidates must appear and speak in their own political commercials.
17. Political advertisements must indicate major contributors and professional groups involved.
18. Newspapers to print periodic, at least monthly, summaries of legislator's activity and votes in local, state and national assemblies - a political page.

* * *

· CHAPTER NOTES ·

CHAPTER I — "The Common Good" —

1. Rossiter, Clinton. The Federalist Papers. Mentor - New American Library. New York. 1961. #57, p. 350.
2. Jefferson, Thomas. Peter's Quotations - Ideas For Our Time. Dr. Lawrence J. Peter. Bantam Books, New York. 1977.
3. Casson, Lionel. And Never Say No: Politics as usaul in Ancient Rome. Smithsonian Magazine. June 1987.
4. Nader, Ralph. Who Runs Congress? Mark Green, James M. Fallows, David R. Zwick. Bantam/Grossman Book. New York. 1972.
5. Rossiter, #78, p. 469.
6. Declaration of Independence.
7. Rossiter, #15, p. 105.
8. Mintz, Morton & Jerry S. Cohen. America Inc. Dell Publishing. New York. 1971. p. 258.
9. Nader, p. 226.
10. Ibid, p. 242.
11. Rossiter, #71, p. 432.
12. Ibid, #71, p. 432.
13. Mee, Charles L. Jr. The Genius of the People. Harper & Row. New York. 1987. p. 51.
14. Nader, p. 243.
15. Smith, Hedrick. The Power Game - How Washington Works. Random House. New York. 1988. p. 158.
16. Stern, Phillip. The Best Congress Money Can Buy. Pantheon Books, New York. 1988. p. 100.
17. De Tocqueville, Alexis. Democracy in America. A Mentor Book. Richard D. Heffner, Editor. New York. 1956. pp. 60-61.
18. Jones, Charles O. Every Second Year - Congression Behavior and the Second Term. The Brookings Institution. Washington D.C. 1967. p. 3-4.
    Nader, p. 235.
20. Jones, p. 10.
21. Ibid, p. 10.
22. Nader, p. 243.
23. Jones, p. 7.

24. Ibid.
25. Ibid.
26. Peter. p. 227.
27. Gallagher, The Accountant.
28. Rossiter, Fed. #71 p. 434.
29. Ibid.
30. Ibid, Fed. #37, p. 227.
31. Ibid, Fed. #72, pp. 436-437.
32. Ibid.
33. Ibid.
34. Ibid. p. 439.
35. Ibid. p. 439.
36. Ibid. p. 440.
37. Ibid, Fed #51, p. 322.
38. Daly, John Charles. How Long Should They Serve? American Enterprise Institute - AEI Forums. April 17, 1980. Washington D.C. 1980. pp. 6.
39. Hartnett, Thomas F. Wall Street Journal. September 19, 1988
40. United States Constitution, Article V.
41. Peter, p. 453.
42. Wallechinsky, David & Irving Wallace. The People's Almanac #3. Bantam Books, New York. 1981. p. 37.
43. Butler, David & Austin Ranney. Referendums. American Enterprise Institute. Washington D.C.. 1978. p. 75-80
44. Ibid.
45. U.S. Constitution.
46. Wallenchinsky, p. 34.
47. Butler, p. 75.
48. Wallechinsky, p. 36.
49. Ibid.
50. Ibid, p. 38.
51. Sorensen, Theodore C. A Different Kind of Presidency - A Proposal for Breaking the Political Deadlock. Harper & Row. New York. 1984. p. 54.
52. Ibid.
53. Ibid. p. 110.
54. Rossiter, Fed. #51, p. 323.
55. Peter, p. 220.
56. Treen, David. Can You Afford This House. Green Hill Publishers, Inc. New Jersey. 1978. p. 21.
57. Ibid, p. 20.
58. Rossiter, Fed. #57, p. 351.
59. Ibid, Fed.#14, p. 104.
60. Ibid.
61. Larsen, Leonard. Santa Ana Register. March 6, 1988.
62. Ibid.
63. Casson, Lionel. And Never Say No: Politics as usaul in Ancient Rome. Smithsonian Magazine. June 1987. p. 54.

CHAPTER II — Corruption and Reelection —

1. Mintz & Cohen. p. 2.
2. Ibid.
3. Shannon, James. Rep. Time Magazine. October 25, 1982. p. 41.
4. Smith, The Power Game. p. 263.
5. Buchanan, Patrick. Santa Ana Register. March 3, 1988. p. 6.
6. Time Magazine, March 25, 1982.
7. Keim, George. Big Business Finds Resource in Own Employees. Los Angeles Times. April 4, 1988.
8. McNeil-Lehrer Report. Public Television. March 1, 1988.
9. Time Magazine, March 25, 1982.
10. Anderson, Jack & Drew Pearson. The Case Against Congress. Simon & Schuster. New York. 1968. p. 12.
11. Winter-Berger, Robert. The Washington Pay-off. Dell Publishing Co. New York. 1972. p. 305.
12. Ibid.
13. Etzioni, Amitai. Capital Corruption - The New Attack On American Democracy. Harcourt Brace Jovanovitch. New York. 1984. p. 68.
14. Paddock, Richard. Los Angeles Times. April 4, 1988.
15. Smith, The Power Game. p. 261.
16. Stern. Best Congress Money Can Buy. p. 75.
17. Steel, Eric. Los Angeles Times. March 2, 1988.
18. Jacobs, Paul. Los Angeles Times. May 18, 1987.
19. Ibid.
20. Ibid.
21. Skeleton, George. Los Angeles Times, Sept. 5, 1988. p. 1.
22. Common Cause Magazine. Sheila Kaplan, Ed. Common Cause. Washington D.C. January/February 1988.
23. Ibid.
24. U.S. Constitution.
25. Common Cause, p. 18.
26. Ibid.
27. Etzioni. Capitol Corruption. pp. 3-5.
28. Ibid.
29. Ibid. p. 59.
30. Ibid.
32. Ibid. p. 69.
33. Common Cause Magazine, Jan '88 p. 23.
34. Smith. The Power Game. p. 119.
35. Common Cause Magazine. May 27, 1987. p. 36.
36. Ibid.
37. Ibid.
38. Burt Neuborn & Arthur Eisenberg. The Rights of Candidates and Voters. American Civil Liberties Union. Avon Books. New York. 1976. pp. 95-97.

39. Ibid.
40. Ibid.
41. Ibid.
42. Ibid. pp. 109-111.
43. Winter-Berger, Robert. The Washington Pay-off. Dell Publishing Co. New York. 1972. p. 12.
44. Ibid. p. 301.
45. Stern. Best Congress Money Can Buy. p. 16.
46. Common Cause Magazine. Jan '88, p. 24.
47. Los Angeles Times, May 22, 1988.
48. Smith. The Power Game. p. 226.
49. Newborn & Eisenberg. A.C.L.U. p. 98.
50. Common Cause Magazine, Jan '88, p. 25.
51. Newbron & Eisenberg. A.C.L.U. p. 96.
52. Stern. p. 191.

CHAPTER III — The Human Nature of Politics —

1. Mee, Charles L. Jr. The Genius of the People. Harper & Row. New York. 1987. p. 124.
2. Ibid.
3. Ibid. p. 223.
4. De Tocqueville. p. 262.
5. Ibid. pp. 164-165.
6. Deakin, James. Straight Stuff. Forbes Magazine April 4, 1988. p. 22.
7. Smith. The Power Game. p. 141.
8. Time Magazine. Dec. 3, 1984. p. 43.
9. Ni, Hua-Ching. The Complete Works of Lao Tzu. The Shrine of the Eternal Breath of Tao. Malibu, Ca. 1979. pp. 177, 199.
10. Ibid.
11. Rouse, W.H,D. Great Dialogues of Plato - The Republic, Book IV. Mentor - New American Library, New York, 1956. p. 224.
12. Rooney, Andy. Santa Ana Register - Cathy Lawhon. March 8, 1988.
13. Nader. p. 210.
14. Mee, p. 220.
15. Peter, p. 416.
16. Vaughn, Francis. The Inward Arc. Yoga Journal, Nov. Dec. 1986.
17. Rouse. p. 146.
18. Lawhon, Cathy. Santa Ana Register. March 8, 1988.
19. Ibid.
20. Ibid.
21. Ibid.
22. Smith. The Power Game. p. 107.
23. Ibid. p. 108.
24. Ibid. p. 113.

CHAPTER IV — Career Bureaucracy and Civil Service Reform

1. Treen. p. 41.
2. Ibid. pp. 41-43.
3. De Tocqueville, p. 303.
4. Ni, Hua-Ching. p. 57.
5. Noah, Timothy. How to End the Federal Pension Scandal. Washington Monthly. May 17, 1985. p. 10.
6. U.S. News & World Report. September 30, 1985. p. 80.
7. Sergei Plekhanov. Los Angeles Times.
8. Santa Ana Register. U.S. Help Wanted. Assoc. Press. Sept. 30, 1988 p. E1.
9. Ibid.
10. Nader, pp. 245.
11. Kotz, Nick. Technology Review. Money, Politics, and the B-1 Bomber. April, 1988. p. 40.
12. Wall St. Journal. May 13, 1988. p. 17B.
13. Ashworth, William. Under The Influence - Congress, Lobbies and the American Pork-Barrel System. Hawthorn/Dutton. New York. 1981. p. 45.
14. Ibid. p. xiii.
15. DeTocqueville, pp. 124-127.
16. Bolling, Richard. House Out of Order. p. 45.
17. Peter, p. 289.
18. Forbes Magazine. April, 1988. p. 14.
19. Ibid.
20. Peter, p. 292.
21. Santa Ana Register editorial. Oct. 4, 1988.
22. Ibid.
23. Chapman, Stephen. Senate Applies Ethics law to Itself. Santa Ana Register. May 1, 1988.
24. Los Angeles Times. September 21, 1987. p. 13.

CHAPTER V — "We, the People" —

1. Mee, Charles. p. 138.
2. California State Department of Education. "You 've Got the Power." p. 1.
3. Moran, Mark Edward. Los Angeles Times. Sept 23, 1988. p. 11.
4. DeTocqueville. pp. 117-118.
5. Los Angeles Times. Opening The Debate. Oct. 2, 1988.
6. Mee, Charles. pp. 50-51.
7. Ibid. p. 262.
8. Krinsky, Fred. Crisis And Innovation - Constitutional Democracy In America. Blackwell, Inc. New York. 1988. p. 56.
9. Mee, p. 138.

10. Salmore, Stephen A. & Barbara G. Salmore. Candidates, Paries, and Campaigns - Electoral Politics in America. CQ Press, Inc. Washington D.C. 1985. p. 428.
11. Ibid. p. 225.
12. Whitridge, Frederick. Politics and People - The Ordeal of Self-Government in America. (Leon Stein, Ed.) Arno Press. New York. 1974. p. 26.
13. Ibid.
14. Ibid. p. 94.
15. Ibid. p. 95.
16. Ibid. p. 59.
17. Rossiter, Fed#68. p. 413.
18. U.S. constitution.
19. Sayre, Wallace & Judith Parris. Voting For President - The Electoral College and the American Political System. The Brookings Institution. Washington,D.C. 1970. p. 9.
20. Ibid. p. 7.
21. Ibid. p. 58.
22. Ibid. p. 49.
23. Ibid. p. 29.
24. Ibid. p. 69.
25. Ibid. p. 102.
26. Rossiter, Fed.#36. p. 217.
27. Orange County Register. You Can 't Tell A President By His Resume. Octeober 5, 1988. p. B11.
28. Frantzich, Stephen. Computers in Congress - The Politics of Information. Sage Publications. Beverly Hills. 1982. p. 15.
29. Ibid. p. 9.
30. Ibid. p. 10.
31. Ibid. p. 46.
32. Ibid.
33. A.C.L.U. - Newborne & Eisenberg. p. 60-70.

CHAPTER VI — Justice For Sale —

1. Common Cause Magazine. p. 30.
2. Ibid.
3. Ibid.
4. Ibid. pp. 28-31/
5. Ibid.
5. Ibid. p. 31.
6. Ibid.
7. Ibid.
8. Ibid.
9. Rossiter, Fed #79 p. 472.

CHAPTER VII — The Media and Politics —

1. Salmore, p. 145.
2. Stern, p. 114.
3. Peter, p. 165
4. Santa Ana Register. August 28, 1988 p. 12.
5. Stern. p. 187.
6. Ibid.
7. Moran, Mark Edward. L.A. Times. Sept. 23, 1988. p. 11.
8. Rouse. p. 224.
9. Wall St. Journal. MAy 13, 1988 p 23

CHAPTER VIII — Conclusions and Recommendations —

1. Bezold, Clement, Ed. Anticipatory Democracy - People in the Politics of the future. Random House. New York. 1978. p. 361.
2. Ibid. pp. 362-365.
3. Ibid. p. 105.

* * *

APPENDIX

CONSTITUTION OF THE UNITED STATES

We the people of the United States, in order to form a more perfect Union, establish Justice, insure domestic tranquility, provide for the common defence, promote the general welfare, and secure the blessings of liberty to ourselves and our Posterity, do ordain and establish this Constitution for the United States of America.

ARTICLE I.

SECTION 1. All legislative powers herein granted shall be vested in a Congress of the United States, which shall consist of a Senate and House of Representatives.

SECTION 2. The House of Representatives shall be composed of Members chosen every second year by the People of the several states, and the Electors in each state shall have the qualifications requisite for Electors of the most numerous Branch of the State legislature.

No Person shall be a Representative who shall not have attained to the Age of twenty-five years, and been seven years a Citizen of the United States, and who shall not, when elected, be an inhabitant of that state in which he shall be chosen.

[Representatives and direct taxes shall be apportioned among the several states which may be included within this union, according to their respective numbers, which shall be determined by adding to the whole number of free persons, including those bound to Service for a term of years, and excluding Indians not taxed, three fifths of all other persons.]* The actual Enumeration shall be made within three years after the first Meeting of the Congress of the United States, and within every subsequent Term of ten years, in such Manner as they shall by law direct. The number of Representatives shall not exceed one for every thirty thousand, but each state shall have at least one representatives, and until such enumeration shall be made, the state of New Hampshire shall be entitled to choose three, Massachusetts eight, Rhode Island and Providence Plantations one, Connecticut five, New York six, New Jersey four, Pennsylvania eight, Delaware one, Maryland six, Virginia ten, North Carolina five, South Carolina fice, and Georgia three.

When vacancies happen in the Representation from any state, the executive Authority thereof shall issue Writs of Election to fill such vacancies.

The House of Representatives shall chuse their Speaker and other Officers; and shall have the sole Power of Impeachment.

 * [Changed by Section 2 of the Fourteenth Amendment]

SECTION 3. The Senate of the United States shall be composed of two Senators from each state, [chosen by the legislature thereof,]* for six years; and each Senator shall have one vote.

Immediately after they shall be assembled in Consequence of the first Election, they shall be divided as equally as may be into three Classes. The Seats of the Senators of the first Class shall be vacated at the Expiration of the second Year, of the second Class at the Expiration of the fourth Year, and of the third class at the Expiration of the sixth Year, so that one third may be chosen every second year; [and if Vacancies happen by Resignation, or otherwise, during the Recess of the Legislature of any State, the Executive thereof may make temporaary Appointments until the next Meeting of the Legislature; which shall then fill such Vacancies.]**

No Person shall be a Senator who shall not have attained to the Age of thirty years, and been nine years a Citizen of the United States, and who shall not, when elected, be an Inhabitant of that State for which he shall be chosen.

The Vice President of the United Stated shall be President of the Senate, but shall have not vote, unless they be equally divided.

The Senate shall chuse their other Officers, and also a President pro tempore, in the Absence of the Vice President, or when he shall exercise the Office of the President of the United States.

The Senate shall have the sole Power to try all Impeachments. When sitting for that purpose, they shall be on Oath or Affirmation. When the President of the United States is tried, the Chief Justice shall preside. And no Person shall be convicted without the Concurrence of two thirds of the Members present.

Judgment in Cases of Impeachment shall not extend further than to removal from Office, and disqualification to hold and enjoy any Office of honor, Trust or Profit under the United States: but the Party convicted shall nevertheless be liable and subject to Indictment, Trial, Judgment and Punishment, according to Law.

 *, * * [Changed by the Seventeenth Amendment]

SECTION 4. The Times, Places, and Manner of holding Elections for Senators and Representatives, shall be prescribed in each State by the Legislature thereof;

but the Congress may at any time by Law make or alter such Regulations, except as to the Places of chusing Senators.

The Congress shall assemble at least once in every Year, and such meeting shall be [on the first Monday in December,]* unless they shall by law appoint a different Day.

* [Changed by Section 2 of the Twentieth Amendment]

SECTION 5. Each House shall be the Judge of the Elections, Returns and Qualificatinos of its own Members, and a Majority of each shall constitute a Quorum to do Business; but a smaller number may adjourn from day to day, and may be authorized to compel the Attendance of absent Members, in such Manner, and under such Penalties as each House may provide.

Each House may determine the Rules of its Proceedings, punish its Members for disorderly Behavior, and, with the Concurrence of two thirds, expel a member.

Each House shall keep a Journal of its Proceedings, and from time to time publish the same, excepting such parts as may in their judgment require Secrecy; and the yeas and nays of the Members of either House on any question shall, at the desire of one fifth of those Present, be entered on the Journal.

Neither House, during the session of Congress, shall, without the Consent of the other, adjourn for more than three days, nor to any other Place than that in which the two Houses shall be sitting.

SECTION 6. The Senators and Representatives shall receive a Compensation for their Services, to be ascertained by law, and paid out of the Treasury of the United States. They shall in all Cases, except Treason, Felony and Breach of the Peace, be privileged from Arrest during their Attendance at the Session of their respective Housess, and in going to and returning from the same; and for any Speech or Debate in either House, they shall not be questioned in any other PLace.

No Representatives shall, during the Time for which he was elected, be appointed to any civil Office under the Authority of the United States, which shall have been created, or the Emoluments whereof shall have been encreased during such time; and no Person holding any Office under the United States, shall be a Member of either House during Continuance in Office.

SECTION 7. All Bills for raising Revenue shall originate in the House of Representatives; but the Senate may propose or concur with Amendments as on other Bills.

Every Bill which shall have passed the House of Representatives and the Senate, shall, before it becomes a law, be presented to the President of the United States; If he approves he shall sign it, but if not he shall return it, with his Objections to that House in which it shall have originated, who shall enter the Objections at large on their Journal, and proceed to reconsider it. If after such Reconsideration two thirds of that House shall agree to pass the Bill, it shall be sent, together with the Objections, to the other House, by which it shall likewise be reconsidered, and if approved by two thirds of that House, it shall become a Law. But in all such Cases the Votes of both Houses shall be determined by yeas and nays, and the Names of Persons voting for and against the Bill shall be entered on the Journal of each House respectively. If any Bill shall not be returned by the President within ten Days (Sundays excepted) after it shall have been presented to him, the Same shall be a law, in like Manner as if he had signed it, unless the Congress by their Adjournment prevent its return, in which Case it shall not be a Law.

Every Order, Resolution, or Vote to which the Concurrence of the Senate and House of Representatives may be necessary (except on a question of Adjournment) shall be presented to the President of the United States; and before the Same shall take Effect, shall be approved by him, or being disapproved by him, shall be repassed by two thirds of the Seante and House of Representatives, according to the Rules and Limitations prescribed in the Case of a Bill.

SECTION 8. The Congress shall have the Power to lay and collect Taxes, Duties, Imposts, and Excises, to pay the Debts and provide for the common Defence and general Welfare of the United States; but all duties, Imposts and excises shall be uniform throughout the United States;

To borrow Money on the credit of the United States;

To regulate Commerce with foreign Nations, and among the several States, and with the Indian Tribes;

To establish a uniform Rule of Naturalization, and uniform Laws on the subject of Bankruptcies throughout the United States;

To coin Money, regulate the value thereof, and of foreign coin, and fix the Standard of Weights and Measures;

To provide for the Punishment of counterfeiting the Securities and current Coin of the United States;

To Establish Post Offices and post roads;

To promote the Progress of Science and useful Arts, by securing for limited Times to authors and Inventors the exclusive Right to their respective Writings and Discoveries;

To constitute Tribunals inferior to the Supreme Court;

To define and punish Piracies and Felonies committed on the high seas, and Offenses against the Law of Nations;

To declare War, grant Letters of Marque and Reprisal, and make Rules concerning Captures on Land and Water;

To raise and support Armies, but no Appropriation of Money to that Use shall be for a longer Term than two years;

To provide and maintain a Navy;

To make rules for the Government and Regulation of the land and naval forces;

To provide for calling forth the Militia to execute the Laws of the Union, suppress insurrection and repel invasions;

To provide for organizing, arming, and disciplining, the Militia, and for governing such Part of them as may be employed in the service of the United States, reserving to the States respectively, the appointment of the Officers, and the Authority of training the Militia according to the discipline prescribed by Congress;

To exercise exclusive Legislation in all cases whatsoever, over such District (not exceeding ten square miles) as may, by Cession of particular States, and the Acceptance of Congress, become the Seat of the Government of the United States, and to exercise like Authority over all Places purchased by the Consent of the Legislature of the State in which the Same shall be, for the Erection of Forts, Magazines, Arsenals, dock-yards and other needful buildings;-And

To make all laws which shall be necessary and proper for carrying into Execution the foregoing Powers, and all other Powers vested by this Constitution in the Goverment of the United States, or in any Department or Officer thereof.

SECTION 9. The Migration or Importation of such Persons as any of the States now existing shall think proper to admit, shall not be prohibited by the Congress prior to the Year one thousand eight, hundred and eight, but a Tax or duty may be imposed on such Importation, not exceeding ten dollars for each Person.

The Privilege of the Writ of Habeas Corpus shall not be suspended, unless when in Cases of Rebellion or Invasion the public Safety may require it.

No Bill of Attainder or ex post facto Law shall be passed.

[No Capitation, or other direct, Tax shall be laid, unless in Proortion to the Census or Enumeration herein before directed to be taken.]*

No Tax or Duty shall be laid on Articles exported from any State.

No Preference shall be given to any Regulation of Commerce or Revenue to the Ports of one State over those of another: nor shall Vessels bound to, or from, one State, be obliged to enter, clear, or pay Duties in another.

No Money shall be drawn from the Treasury, but in Consequence of Appropriations made by Law; and a regular Statement and Account of the Receipts and Expenditures of all public Money shall be published from time to time.

No Title of Nobility shall be granted by the United States; And no Person holding any Office of profit under them, shall, without the Consent of the Congress, accept of any present, Emolument, Office, or Title, of any kind whatsoever, from any King, Prince, or foreign State.

* [Changed by the Sixteenth Amendment]

SECTION 10. No State shall enter into any Treasury, Alliance, or Confederation; grant Letters of Marque and Reprisal; coin Money; emit Bills of Credit; make any Thing but gold and silver coin a tender in Payment of Debts; pass any Bill of Attainder, ex post facto Law, or Law impairing the Obligation of Contracts, or grant any Title of Nobility.

No State shall, without the Consent of the Congress, lay any Imposts or Duties on Imports or Exports, except what may be absolutely necessary for executing its inspection Laws: and the net Produce of all Duties and Imposts, laid by any State on Imports or Exports, shall be for the Use of the Treasury of the United States; and all such laws shall be subject to the Revision and Control of the Congress.

No State shall, without the Consent of Congress, lay any Duty of Tonnage, keep Troops, or Ships of War in time of Peace, enter into any Agreement or Compact with another State, or with a foreign Power, or engage in War, unless actually invaded, or in such imminent Danger as will not admit of delay.

ARTICLE II.

SECTION 1. The executive Power shall be vested in a President of the United States of America. He shall hold his Office during the Term of four Years, and, together with the Vice President, chosen for the same term, be elected, as follows.

Each State shall appoint, in such Manner as the Legislature thereof may direct, a Number of Electors, equal to the whole Number of Senators and Representatives to which the State may be entitled in the Congress; but no Senator or Representative, or person holding an Office of Trust or Profit under the United States, shall be appointed an Elector.

[The Electors shall meet in their respective States, and vote by Ballot for two Persons, of whom one at least shall not be an inhabitant of the same State with themselves. And they shall make a list of all the Persons voted for, and of the Number of Votes for each; which List they shall sign and certify, and transmit sealed to the Seat of the Government of the United States, directed to the President of the Senate. The President of the Senate shall, in the presence of the Senate and House of Representatives, open all the certificates, and the Votes shall then be counted. The Person having the greatest Number of Votes shall be the President, if such Number be a Majority of the whole Number of Electors appointed; and if there be more than one who have such Majority, and have an equal number of Votes, then the House of Representatives shall immediately chuse by Ballot one of them for President; and if no Person have a Majority, then from the five highest on the List the said House shall in like manner chuse the President. But in chusing the President, the Votes shall be taken by States, the Representation from each State having one vote; A Quorum for this purpose shall consist of a Member or Members from two thirds of the states, and a majority of all the States shall be necessary to a Choice. In every Case, after the Choice of the President, the Person having the greatest number of Votes of the Electors shall be the Vice President. But if there should remain two or more who have equal Votes, the Seante shall chuse from them by Ballot the Vice President.]*

218

The Congress may determine the Time of chusing the Electors, and the Day on which they shall give their Votes; which Day shall be the same throughout the United States.

No Person except a natural born Citizen, or a Citizen of the United States, at the time of the Adoption of this Constitution, shall be eligible to the Office of the President; neither shall any person be eligible to that Office who shall not have attained to the Age of thirty five years, and been fourteen Years a Resident within the United States.

[In case of the Removal of the President from Office, or of his death, Resignation, or Inability to discharge the Power and Duties of the said Office, the same shall devolve on the Vice President, and the Congress may by law provide for the Case of Removal, Death, Resignation or inability, both of the President and Vice President, declaring what officer shall then act as President, and such Officer shall act accordingly, until the Disability be removed, or a President shall be elected.]**

The President shall, at stated times, receive for his Services, a Compensation, which shall neither be increased nor diminished during the Period for which he shall have been elected, and he shall not receive within that Period any other Emolument from the United States, or any of them.

Before he enters the Execution of his Office, he shall take the following Oath or Affirmation: - "I do solemnly swear (or affirm) that I will faithfully execute the Office of President of the United States, and will to the best of my Ability, preserve, protect, and defend the Constitution of the United States."

*   [Changed by the Twelfth Amendment]
** [Changed by the Twenty-fifth Amendment]

SECTION 2. The President shall be Commander in Chief of the Army and Navy of the United States, and of the Militia of the several States, when called into the actual Service of the United States; he may require the Opinion, in writing, of the Principal Officer in each of the executive Departments, upon any subject relating to the Duties of their respective Offices, and he shall have the Power to grant Reprieves and Pardons for Offenses against the United States, except in cases of Impeachment.

He shall have the Power, by and with the Advice and Consent of the Senate, to make Treaties, provided two thirds of the Senators present concur; and he shall nominate; and by and with the Advice and Consent of the Senate, shall appoint Ambassadors, other public Ministers and Consuls, Judges of the Supreme Court, and alll other Officers of the United States, whose Appointments are not herein otherwise provide for, and which shall be established by Law: but the Congress may by Law vest the Appointment of such inferior Officers, as they think proper, in the President alone, in the Courts of Law, or in the Heads of Departments.

The President shall have the Power to fill up all Vacancies that may happen during the Recess of the Senate, by granting Commissions which shall expire at the End of their next session.

SECTION 3. He shall from time to time give to the Congress Information of the State of the Union, and recommend to their Consideration such Measures as he shall judge necessary and expedient; he may, on extraordinary Occasions, convene both Houses, or either of them, and in Case of Disagreement between them, with Respect to the Time of Adjournment, he may adjourn them to such Time as he shall think proper; he shall receive Ambassadors and other public Ministers; he shall take care that the laws be faithfully executed, and shall Commission all the Officers of the United States.

SECTION 4. The President, Vice President and all civil Officers of the United States, shall be removed from Office on Impeachment for, and Conviction of, Treason, Bribery, or other high Crimes and Misdemeanors.

ARTICLE III.

SECTION 1. The Judicial Power of the United States, shall be vested in one supreme Court, and in such inferior Courts as the Congress may from time to time ordain and establish. The Judges, both of the supreme and inferior Courts, shall hold their Offices during good Behavior, and shall, at stated Times, receive for their Services, a Compensation, which shall not be diminshed during their continuance in Office.

SECTION 2. The judicial Power shall extend to all Cases, in Law and Equity, arising under this Constitution, the Laws of the United States, and Treaties made, or which shall be made, under their Authority; - to all Cases affecting Ambassadors, other public Ministers and Consuls; - to all Cases of Admiralty and maritime Jurisdiction; to controversies to which the United States shall be a Party; to Controversies between two or more States; [Between a State and Citizens of another state;]* between Citizens of different States - between Grants of different States, [and between a State, or the Citizens thereof, and foreign States, Citizens or Subjects.]*

In all Cases affecting Ambassadors, other public Ministers and Consuls, and those in which a State shall be a Party, the supreme Court shall have the original Jurisdiction. In all the other Cases before mentioned, the supreme Court shall have appellate Jurisdiction, both as to Law and Fact, with such Exceptions, and under such Regulations as the Congress shall make.

The Trial of all Crimes, except in Cases of Impeachment; shall be by Jury; and such Trial shall be held in the State where the said Crimes shall have been committed; but whn not committed within any state, the Trial shall be at such Place or Places as the Congress may by Law have directed.

* [Changed by the Eleventh Amendment]

SECTION 3. Treason Against the United States, shall consist only in levying War against them, or in adhering to their Enemies, giving them Aid and Comfort. No Person shall be convicted of Treason unless on the Testimony of two Witnesses to the same overt Act, or on Confession in open Court.

The Congress shall have the Power to declare the Punishment of Treason, but no Attainder of Treason shall work Corruption of Blood, or Forfeiture except during the Life of the Person attainted.

ARTICLE IV.

SECTION 1. Full Faith and Credit shall be given each State to the public Acts, Records, and judicial Proceedings of every other State; And the Congress may by general Laws prescribe the Manner in which such Acts, Records and Proceedings shall be proved, and the Effect thereof.

SECTION 2. The Citizens of each State shall be entitled to all Privileges and Immmunities of Citizens in the several States.

A Person charged in any state with Treason, Felony, or other Crime, who shall flee from Justice, and be found in another State, shall on Demand of the executive Authority of the State from which he fled, be delivered up, to be removed to the State having Jurisdiction of the Crime.

[No Person held to Service of Labour in one State, under the Laws thereof, escaping into another, shall, in consequence of any Law or Regulation therein, be discharged from such Service or labour, but shall be delivered up on Claim of the Party to whom such Service of Labour may be due.]*

* [Changed by the Thirteenth Amendment]

SECTION 3. New States may be admitted by the Congress into this Union; but no new State shall be formed or erected within the Jurisdiction of any other State; nor any state be formed by the Junction of Two or more state, or Parts of States, without the Consent of the Legislatures of the States concerned as well as of the Congress.

The congress shall have Power to dispose of and make all needful Rules and Regulations respecting the Terrritory or other Property belonging to the United States; and nothing in this Constitution shall be so construed as to Prejudice any Claims of the United States, or of any particular State.

SECTION 4. The United States Shall Guarantee to every State in this Union a Republican Form of Government, and shall protect each of them against Invasion; and on application of the Legislature, or of the Executive (when the Legislature cannot be convened) against domestic Violence.

ARTICLE V.

The Congress, whenever two thirds of both Houses shall deem it necessary, shall propose Amendments to this Constitution, or, on the Application of the Legislatures of two-thirds of the several States, shall call a Convention for proposing Amendments, which, in either case, shall be valid to all Intents and Purposes, as Part of this Constitution, when ratified by the Legislatures of three-fourths of the several States, or by Conventions in three-fourths thereof, as the one of the other mode of Ratification may be proposed by the Congress; Provided that no Amendment which may be made prior to the Year One thousand eight hundred and eight shall in any Manner affect the first and fourth Clauses in the Ninth Section of the first Article; and that no State, without its Consent, shall be deprived of it's equal Suffrage in the Senate.

ARTICLE VI.

All Debts contracted and Engagements entered into, before the Adoption of this Constitution, shall be as valid against the United States under this Constitution, as under the Confederation.

This Constitution, and the Laws of the United States which shall be made in Pursuance thereof; and all Treaties made, or which shall be made, under the Authority of the United States, shall be the supreme Law of the Land; and the Judges in every State shall be bound thereby, and any thing in the Constitution or Laws of any State to the contrary notwithstanding.

The Senators and Representatives before mentioned, and the members of the several State Legislature, and all executive and judicial Officers, both of the United States and of the several State, shall be bound by Oath or Affirmation, to support this Constitution; but not religious Test shall ever by required as a Qualification of any Office or Public Trust under the United States.

ARTICLE VII.

The Ratification of the Convention of Nine States, shall be sufficient for the establishment of this Constitution between the States so ratifying the Same.

Done in Convention by the Unanimous Consent of the States present the Seventeenth Day of September in the Year of our Lord one Thousand seven hundred and Eight seven and of the Independence of the United States of America the Twelfth in Witness whereof We have hereunto subscribed our Names,

G. Washington, President
and Deputy from Virginia

AMENDMENTS TO THE CONSTITUTION
OF THE UNITED STATES

AMENDMENT I

Congress shall make no law respecting an establishment of religion, or prohibiting the free exercise thereof; or abridging the freedom of speech, or of the press, or the right of the people peaceably to assemble, and to petition the Government for a redress of grievances.

AMENDMENT II

A well regulated Militia, being necessary to the security of a free State, the right of the people to keep and bear arms, shall not be infringed.

AMENDMENT III

No Soldier shall, in time of peace be quartered in any house, without the consent of the Owner, nor in time of war, but in a manner to be prescribed by law.

AMENDMENT IV

The right of the people to be secure in their persons, houses, papers, and effects, against unreasonable searches and seizures, shall not be violated, and no warrants shall issue, but upon probable cause, supported by Oath or affirmation, and particularly describing the place to be searched, and the persons or things to be seized.

AMENDMENT V

No person shall be held to answer for a capital, or otherwise infamous crime, unless on a presentment or indictment of a Grand Jury, except in cases arising in the land or naval forces, or in the Militia, when in actual service in time of War or public danger; nor shall any person be subject for the same offence to be put twice in jeopardy of life or limb, nor shall be compelled in any criminal case to be a witness against himself, nor be deprived of life, liberty, or property, without due process of law; nor shall private property be taken for public use without just compensation.

AMENDMENT VI

In all criminal prosecutions, the accused shall enjoy the right to a speedy and public trial, by an impartial jury of the State and district wherein the crime shall have been committed; which district shall have been previously committed; which district shall have been previously ascertained by law, and to be informed of the nature and cause of the accusation; to be confronted with the witnesses against him; to have compulsory process for obtaining witnesses in his favor, and to have the assistance of counsel for his defence.

AMENDMENT VII

In Suits at common law, where the value in controvery shall exceed twenty dollars, the right of trial by jury shall be preserved, and no fact tried by a jury shall be otherwise re-examined in any Court of the United States, than according to the rules of the common law.

AMENDMENT VIII

Excessive bail shall not be required, nor excessive fines imposed, nor cruel and unusual punishments inflicted.

AMENDMENT IX

The enumeration in the Constitution of certain rights shall not be construed to deny or disparage others retained by the people.

AMENDMENT X

The powers not delegated to the United States by the Constitution, nor prohibited by it to the State, are reserved to the States respectively, or to the people.

**** The first ten amendments to the Constitution - The Bill of Rights - were ratified effective December 15, 1791.

AMENDMENT XI (1795)

The Judicial power of the United States shall not be construed to extend to any suit in law or equity, commenced or prosecuted against one of the United States by Citizens of another State, or by Citizens or Subjects of any foreign State.

AMENDMENT XII (1804)

The Electors shall meet in their respective states, and vote by ballot for President and Vice President, one of whom, at least, shall not be an inhabitant of the same state with themselves; they shall name in their ballots the person voted for as President, and in distinct ballots the person voted for as Vice-President, and they shall make distinct lists of all persons voted for as President, and of all persons voted for as Vice-President, and of the number of votes of each, which lists they shall sign and certify, and transmit sealed to the seat of the government of the United States, directed to the President of the Senate;- The President of the Senate shall, in the presence of the Senate and House of Representatives, open all the certificates and the votes shall then be counted; - The person having the greatest number of votes for President, shall be the President, if such number be a majority of the whole number of Electors appointed; and if no person have such majority, then from the persons having the highest numbers not exceeding three on the list of those voted for as President, the House of Representatives shall choose immediately, by ballot, the President. But in choosing the President, the votes shall be taken by states, the representation from each state having one vote; a quorum for this purpose shall consist of a member or members from two-thirds of the states, and a majority of all the state shall be necessary to a choice. [And if the House of Representatives shall not choose a President whenever the right of choice shall devolve upon them, before the fourth day of March next following, then the Vice-President shall act as President, as in the case of the death or other constitutional disability of the President.]* The person having the greatest number of votes as Vice-President shall be the Vice-President, if such number be a majority of the whole number of Electors appointed, and if no person have a majority, then from the two highest numbers on the list, the Senate shall choose the Vice-President; a quorum for the purpose shall consist of two-thirds of the whole number of Senators, and a majority of the whole number shall be necessary to a choice. But no person constitutionally ineligible to the office of President shall be eligible to that of Vice-President of the United States.

* [Superseded by section 3 of Twentieth Amendment.]

AMENDMENT XIII (1865)

Section 1. Neither slavery not involuntary servitude, except as punishment for crimes whereof the party shall have been duly convicted, shall exist within the United States, or any place subject to their jurisdiction.

Section 2. Congress shall have power to enforce this article by appropriate legislation.

AMENDMENT XIV (1868)

Section 1. All persons born or naturalized in the United States and subject to the jurisdiction thereof, are citizens of the United States and of the state wherein they reside. No State shall make or enforce any law which shall abridge the privileges or immunities of citizens of the United States; not shall any state deprive any person of life, liberty, or property, without due process of law; nor deny to any person within its jurisdiction the equal protection of the laws.

Section 2. Representatives shall be apportioned among the several states according to their respective numbers, counting the whole number of persons in each state, excluding Indians not taxed. But when the right to vote at any election for the choice of electors for President and Vice President of the Uited States, Representatives in Congress, the Executive and Judicial officers of a State, or the members of the Legislature thereof, is denied to any of the male inhabitants of such State, being twenty-one years of age, and citizens of the United States, or in any way abridged, except for participation in rebellion, or other crime, the basis of representation therein shall be reduced in the proportion which the number of such male citizens shall bear to the whole number of male citizens twenty-one years of age in such state.

Section 3. No person shall be a Senator or Representative in Congress, or elector of President and Vice President, or hold any office, civil or military, under the United States, or under any State, who, having previously taken an oath, as a member of any state legislature, or as an executive or judicial officer of any state, to support the Constitution of the United States, shall have engaged in insurrection or rebellion against the same, or given aid or comfort to the enemies thereof. But Congress may by a vote of two-thirds of each house, remove such disability.

Section 4. The validity of the public debt of the United states, authorized by law, including debts incurred for payment of pensions and bounties for services in suppressing insurrection or rebellion, shall not be questioned. But neither the United States nor any state shall assume or pay any debt or obligation incurred in aid of insurrection or rebellion against the United States, or any claim for the loss or emancipation of any slave; but all such debts, obligations and claims shall be held illegal and void.

Section 5. The Congress shall have the power to enforce, by appropriate legislation, the provisions of this article.

AMENDMENT XV (1870)

Section 1. The rights of citizens of the United States to vote shall not be denied or abridged by the United States or by any State on account of race, color, or previous condition of servitude.

Section 2. The Congress shall have the power to enforce this article by appropriate legislation.

AMENDMENT XVI (1913)

The Congress shall have the power to lay and collect taxes on incomes, from whatever source derived, without apportionment among the several states, and without regard to any census or enumeration.

AMENDMENT XVII (1913)

The Senate of the United States shall be composed of two senators from each State, elected by the people thereof, for six years; and each Senator shall have one vote. The Electors in each State shall have the qualifications requisite for electors of the most numerous branch of the State legislatures.

When vacancies happen in the representation of any state in the senate, the executive authority of such state shall issue writs of election to fill such vacancies: Provided, That the legislature of any State may empower the executive thereof to make temporary appointments until the people fill the vacancies by election as the legislature may direct.

This amendment shall not be so construed as to affect the election or term of any Senator chosen before it becomes valid as part of the Constitution.

AMENDMENT XVIII (1919)

[Section 1. After one year from the ratification of this article the manufacture, sale, or transportation of intoxicating liquors within, the importation thereof into, or the exportation thereof from the United States and all territory subject to the jurisdiction thereof for beverage purposes is hereby prohibited.

Section 2. The Congress and the several states shall have concurrent power to enforce this article by appropriate legislation.

Section 3. This article shall be inoperative unless it shall have been ratified as an amendment to the Constitution by the legislatures of the several States, as provided in the Constitution, within seven years from the date of the submission hereof to the States by the Congress.]

* [Repealed by the Twenty-First Amendment]

AMENDMENT XIX (1920)

The rights of citizens of the United States to vote shall not be denied or abridged by the United States or by any state on account of sex.

Congress shall have the power to enforce this article by appropriate legislation.

AMENDMENT XX (1933)

Section 1. The terms of the President and Vice President shall end at noon on the 20th day of January, and the terms of Senators and Representatives at noon on the 3rd day of January, of the years in which such terms would have ended if this article had not been ratified; and the terms of their successors shall then begin.

Section 2. The Congress shall Assemble at least once in every year, and such meeting shall begin at noon on the 3rd day of January, unless they shall by law appoint a different day.

Section 3. If, at the time fixed for the beginning of the term of the President, the President elect shall have died, the Vice President elect shall become President. If a President shall not have been chosen before the time fixed for the beginning of his term, or if the President elect shall have failed to qualify, then the Vice President elect shall act as President until a President shall have qualified; and the Congress may by law provide for the case wherein neither a President elect nor a Vice President elect shall have qualified, declaring who shall then act as President, or the manner in which one who is to act shall be selected, and such person shall act accordingly until a President or Vice President shall have qualified.

Section 4. The Congress may by law provide for the case of the death of any of the persons from whom the House of Representatives may choose a President whenever the right of choice shall have devolved upon them, and for the case of the death of any of the persons from whom the Senate may choose a Vice President whenever the right of choice shall have devolved upon them.

Section 5. Sections 1 and 2 shall take effect on the 15th day of October following the ratification of this article.

Section 6. This article shall be inoperative unless it shall have been ratified as an amendment to the Constitution by the legislatures of three-fourths of the several states within seven years from the date of its submission.

AMENDMENT XXI (1933)

Section 1. The eighteenth article of amendment to the Constitution of the United States is hereby repealed.

Section 2. The transportation or importation into any State, territory, or possession of the United States for delivery or use therein of intoxicating liquors, in violation of the laws thereof, is hereby prohibited.

Section 3. This article shall be inoperative unless it shall have been ratified as an amendment to the Constitution by conventions in the several states, as provided in the Constitution, within seven years from the date of the submission hereof to the States by the Congress.

AMENDMENT XXII (1951)

Section 1. No person shall be elected to the office of the President more than twice, and no person who has held the office of President, or acted as President, for more than two years of a term to which some other person was elected President shall be elected to the office of the President more than once. But his article shall not apply to any person holding the office of President when this article was proposed by the Congress, and shall not prevent any person who may be holding the office of President, or acting as President, during the term within which this Article becomes operative from holding the office of President or acting as President during the remainder of such term.

Section 2. This article shall be inoperative unless it shall have been ratified as an amendment to the Constitution by the legislatures of three-fourths of the several states within seven years from the date of its submission to the states by the Congress.

AMENDMENT XXIII (1961)

Section 1. The District constituting the seat of government of the United States shall appoint in such manner as the Congress may elect: A number of electors of President and Vice President equal to the whole number of Senators and Representatives in Congress to which the District would be entitled if it were a state, but in no event more that the least populous state, they shall be in addition to those appointed by the States. but they shall be considered, for the purposes of the election of President adn Vice President, to be electors appointed by a State; and they shall meet in the district and perform such duties as provided by the twelth article of amendment.

Section 2. The Congress shall have power to enforce this article by appropriate legislation.

AMENDMENT XXIV (1964)

Section 1. The right of citizens of the United States to vote in any primary or other election for President of Vice President, for electors for President or Vice President, or for Senator or Representative in Congress, shall not be denied or abridged by the United States or any State by reason of failure to pay any poll tax or other tax.

Section 2. The Congress shall have the power to enforce this article by appropriate legislation.

AMENDMENT XXV (1967)

Section 1. In case of the removal of the President from office or of his death or resignation, the Vice President shall become President.

Section 2. Whenever there is a vacancy in the office of the Vice President, the President shall nominate a Vice President who shall take office upon confirmation by a majority vote of both Houses of Congress.

Section 3. Whenever the President transmits to the President pro tempore of the Senate and the Speaker of the House of Representatives his written declaration that he is unable to discharge the power and duties of his office, and until he transmits to them a written declaration to the contrary, such powers and duties shall be discharged by the vice president as acting President.

Section 4. Whenever the Vice President and a majority of either the principal officers of the executive departments or of such other body as Congress may by law provide, transmit to the President pro tempore of the Senate and the Speaker of the House of Representatives their written declaration that the President is unable to discharge the powers and duties of his office, the Vice President shall immediately assume the powers and duties of the office as Acting President.

Thereafter, when the President transmits to the President pro tempore of the Senate and the Speaker of the House of Representatives his written declaration that no inability exists, he shall resume the powers and duties of his office unless the Vice President and a majority of either the principal officers of the executive department or of such other body as Congress may be law provide, transmit within four days to the President pro tempore of the Senate and the Speaker of the House of Representatives their written declaration that the President is unable to discharge the power and duties of his office. Thereupon Congress shall decide the issue, assembling within forty-eight hours for that purpose if not in session. If the Congress, within twenty-one days after receipt of the latter written declaration, or, if Congress is not in session, within twenty-one days after Congress is required to assemble, determines by two-thirds vote of both Houses that the President is unable to discharge the powers and duties of his office, the Vice President shall continue to discharge the same as Acting President; otherwise, the President shall resume the powers and duties of his office.

AMENDMENT XXVI (1971)

Section 1. The right of citizens of the United States, who are eighteen years of age or older, to vote shall not be denied or abridged by the United States or by any state on account of age.

Section 2. The Congress shall have power to enforce this article by appropriate legislation.

* * * * *

RATIFICATION OF CONSTITUTION

December	7,	1787	Delaware	30 yeas,	0 nays
December	12,	1787	Pennsylvannia	46 yeas,	23 nays
December	18,	1787	New Jersey	38 yeas,	0 nays
January	2,	1788	Georgia	26 yeas,	0 nays
January	9,	1788	Connecticut	128 yeas,	40 nays
February	6,	1788	Massachusetts	187 yeas,	168 nays
April	28,	1788	Maryland	63 yeas,	11 nays
May	23,	1788	South Carolina	149 yeas,	73 nays
June	21,	1788	New Hampshire	57 yeas,	47 nays

* Constitution ratified after nine state

June	25,	1788	Virginia	89 yeas,	79 nays

* Virginia recommends Bill of right

July	26,	1788	New York	30 yeas,	27 nays
November	21,	1789	North Carolina	194 yeas,	77 nays
May	29,	1790	Rhode Island	34 yeas,	32 nays

* * * * *